THE U.S. GOVERNMENT
HOW IT WORKS

THE HISTORY OF
THE DEMOCRATIC PARTY

THE U.S. GOVERNMENT
HOW IT WORKS

★ ★ ★

THE CENTRAL INTELLIGENCE AGENCY
THE DEPARTMENT OF HOMELAND SECURITY
THE FEDERAL BUREAU OF INVESTIGATION
THE HISTORY OF THE DEMOCRATIC PARTY
THE HISTORY OF THE REPUBLICAN PARTY
THE HISTORY OF THE THIRD PARTIES
THE HOUSE OF REPRESENTATIVES
HOW A LAW IS PASSED
HOW THE CONSTITUTION WAS CREATED
HOW THE PRESIDENT IS ELECTED
THE IMPEACHMENT PROCESS
THE PRESIDENCY
THE SENATE
THE SUPREME COURT

THE U.S. GOVERNMENT
HOW IT WORKS

THE HISTORY OF THE DEMOCRATIC PARTY

HEATHER LEHR WAGNER

CHELSEA HOUSE
P U B L I S H E R S
An imprint of Infobase Publishing

The History of the Democratic Party

Chelsea House
An imprint of Infobase Publishing
132 West 31st Street
New York NY 10001

Library of Congress Cataloging-in-Publication Data
Wagner, Heather Lehr.
 The history of the Democratic Party / Heather Lehr Wagner.
    p. cm. — (The U.S. government)
 Includes bibliographical references and index.
 ISBN-13: 978-0-7910-9419-8 (hardcover)
 ISBN-10: 0-7910-9419-7 (hardcover)
 1. Democratic Party—History.   2. United States—Politics and government.   I. Title.
 JK2316.W34 2007
 324.273609—dc22   2006102363

Chelsea House books are available at special discounts when purchased in bulk quantities for businesses, associations, institutions, or sales promotions. Please call our Special Sales Department in New York at (212) 967-8800 or (800) 322-8755.

You can find Chelsea House on the World Wide Web at
http://www.chelseahouse.com

Text design by James Scotto-Lavino
Cover design by Ben Peterson

Printed in the United States of America

Bang NMSG 10 9 8 7 6 5 4 3 2

This book is printed on acid-free paper.

All links and Web addresses were checked and verified to be correct at the time of publication. Because of the dynamic nature of the Web, some addresses and links may have changed since publication and may no longer be valid.

CONTENTS

1 Party Politics 7

2 Jefferson's Republicans 16

3 A Party Divided 31

4 Slavery and the Democratic Party 47

5 War and Politics 60

6 A New Deal 70

7 Changing Society 83

8 The Modern Democratic Party 96

Glossary .107

Bibliography 110

Further Reading 112

Picture Credits 114

Index 115

About the Author 120

1

PARTY POLITICS

In the earliest years of America's history as an independent nation, the country was unified behind its leadership. George Washington was the unanimous choice as the nation's first president. His cabinet featured many men who had figured prominently in the Continental Congress and the American Revolution, men who had stood firmly united in the effort to win independence from Great Britain.

This spirit of unity and common purpose would not last, however. In Washington's cabinet were men whose differences would soon become so great that they would form political parties to clarify their views and positions on the key issues of the day. One of these issues was precisely how power would be balanced in the new nation. Would the United States have a strong central government or would the greater power remain with the individual state governments?

George Washington's cabinet featured many men who had figured prominently in the American Revolution. The first cabinet is shown above in 1789, left to right: Henry Knox, Thomas Jefferson, Edmund Jennings Randolph, Alexander Hamilton, and George Washington.

Washington's secretary of the treasury, Alexander Hamilton, supported the idea of a strong central government. The political party he formed became known as the Federalist Party. Thomas Jefferson, Washington's secretary of state, believed that a strong central government would quickly become as oppressive to its citizens as the British had been to American colonists. Jefferson favored a government in which the majority of the power would be held by the individual states. Jefferson wanted the new nation to become a republic—a country in which power is held by the voting citizens and by the representatives they choose—and for this reason, his political party was known as the Republican Party.

Soon, other issues sparked greater divisions within Washington's cabinet. First was the question of whether or not the Bill of Rights should be added to the U.S. Constitution. Jefferson's Republicans supported the addition of the Bill of Rights; Hamilton's Federalists opposed it.

Economic policies were another area of disagreement. In the years after the Revolutionary War, America was struggling with debt—debt owed to Americans who had served in the Continental Army and provided it with supplies, as well as debts to foreign nations that had helped with the Revolution. Hamilton thought that the national government should assume the responsibility of paying all war debts, both those of the nation and those of the individual states. Hamilton's plan to pay off these debts involved a tax on imported goods and on certain American-manufactured items, including whiskey. In addition, Hamilton argued for the creation of a national bank—one bank that would oversee the banks of the individual states. Jefferson and his Republicans strongly opposed these economic policies.

Foreign policy was yet another area that sparked debate. As war brewed in Europe, Jefferson and Hamilton disagreed on what America's position should be. In 1790, it was learned that Spanish naval vessels had taken command of British ships off of Vancouver Island in Canada. Jefferson argued that America's position should be one of neutrality: not supporting either side but instead continuing to do business with as many nations as possible. Hamilton disagreed; he eventually met with an agent of the British government in Canada and indicated that America might support Great Britain in the event of war. In 1792, when war broke out between France and Great Britain, the split between the two men widened. Joined by Vice President John Adams, Hamilton argued that America should support Great Britain—its major trading partner—in the conflict. Jefferson felt that America owed a debt to France for its support in the Revolutionary War.

These two powerful men soon persuaded other political leaders to take sides on the issues of the day. Those who, like Jefferson, believed that any powers not specifically granted in the Constitution to the national government should remain under the control of the individual states, were labeled "Republicans." Those who supported Hamilton in his belief that the national government should take whatever steps were necessary for the common good were known as "Federalists."

In 1796, the president and vice president were determined based on who received the largest and second-largest number of electoral votes. Federalist John Adams was elected president, and Republican Thomas Jefferson was elected vice president. The two men had once been good friends, but their very different views about how the government should be run soon created an administration marked more by hostility than by unified purpose. It is difficult to imagine today a situation in which the two leading candidates from different political parties, both running for president, would then be expected to put aside their differences and work together cooperatively as president and vice president, but this is precisely what happened in 1796.

In 1798, the Federalist-controlled Congress passed a highly controversial set of policies known as the Alien and Sedition Acts. The Alien Act gave President Adams the power to expel any foreigners that he felt might threaten national security; it also extended the period of time foreigners needed to live in the United States before they could apply for citizenship. The Sedition Act declared that anyone who published false statements about the president, his government, or Congress could be fined or put in prison.

Jefferson was outraged. He viewed these acts as proof that the United States was moving in the direction of monarchy. He felt that the acts were an attempt to silence political opposition (the majority of those fined and imprisoned under the Sedition Act were Republican newspaper editors) and a violation of the constitutional guarantee of freedom of speech.

Although Jefferson was a member of the government in power, he was determined to focus on strengthening the Republican Party and attempting to win the presidency. At one point, the Federalists had tried to link Jefferson's Republicans with France's "radical democrats"—those whose actions during the French Revolution resulted in widespread violence and terror. The Federalists had sarcastically labeled Jefferson's Republicans "Democratic-Republicans." In 1798, the Republicans adopted this label—"Democratic-Republican Party"—as their official name.

THE ELECTION OF 1800

The election of 1800—in which Thomas Jefferson and another Republican, Aaron Burr, challenged John Adams in his bid for reelection to the presidency—would prove to be one of the most significant in American history. Jefferson had devised his strategy long before the election. Two years earlier, he had begun a letter-writing campaign designed to spread his thoughts around the country. Jefferson sent letters to all of his influential Republican supporters and also to Republican newspapers. In the letters, he explained the reasons behind the political positions he had adopted. He explained why he believed that the powers of the individual states needed to be protected. He also argued against what he felt was an attempt to transfer all of the powers of the states to the federal government and the powers of the federal government to the presidency.

Thomas Jefferson *(above)* challenged John Adams in his bid for reelection in 1800. This was the first U.S. election in which political parties had nominated candidates.

Jefferson's letters called for a smaller, more cost-effective government, one that would use any leftover tax revenue to pay off national debt. He argued against a standing army in peacetime, expressing his belief that state militias were able to provide defense unless the country was invaded. Finally, the letters outlined Jefferson's support for freedom of the press and freedom of religion.

The election of 1800 was also noteworthy for the beginning of what eventually became known as "dirty campaigning." Jefferson, Burr, and Adams avoided directly criticizing each other, but their supporters were not so restrained. The candidates' supporters began using newspapers and pamphlets to criticize the candidates' policies, records, and reputations. Their characters were attacked through gossip and rumors. Jefferson's supporters attacked Adams and the Federalists for deficit spending and for their unfocused foreign policy. Federalists attacked Jefferson's character, labeling him "un-Christian."

When the election was over, John Adams failed to hold on to the presidency. He had received only 65 electoral votes, but Thomas Jefferson and Aaron Burr had tied—each received 73 electoral votes.

Under the terms that then existed in the Constitution, a tie was to be decided in the House of Representatives, which was still dominated by Federalists (the election had changed the balance of power, but the newly elected Republican representatives had not yet taken office). After several days, 36 ballots, and much behind-the-scenes campaigning, Jefferson was finally chosen as the new president. Burr became the vice president.

This was a pivotal moment in American history. Political parties had nominated candidates. Candidates had run on issue platforms. Power had peacefully changed hands from one political party to another. Future presidential campaigns would forever be influenced by these events.

Yet the election of 1800 also marked the end of an era. Before the next presidential election, the Twelfth Amendment to the Constitution would go into effect, changing the presidential electoral process so that electors would cast separate ballots to elect the president and the vice president. Jefferson's Democratic-Republican Party would become the dominant political party in the United States, returning Jefferson to the presidency in 1804, as well as ensuring the election of James Madison in 1808 and 1812 and James Monroe in 1816. By 1820, the Federalist Party—the party that had, in many ways, shaped the national government we know today—had faded away, and James Monroe ran unopposed in his reelection campaign.

The party founded by Thomas Jefferson, the party formed of those who shared his Republican ideals, is today the oldest political party in the United States and is among the oldest political parties in the world. The party originally known as the Republican Party is known today by another name, however: the Democratic Party.

2

Jefferson's Republicans

The victory of Thomas Jefferson and his Republicans over the Federalists in 1801 can be described as a win for his party. It was not simply Jefferson, the candidate, who won the election; the party's successes at publicizing their candidate's views, at campaigning, and at sensing what voters wanted also contributed to the victory.

Because the presidency had never before shifted from one political party to another, there was at first some uncertainty about how this kind of a transition would be handled: For example, would people appointed to positions by the Federalist president, John Adams, keep their jobs? Jefferson was particularly annoyed that Adams had rushed through many appointments just before leaving office.

At first—in his inaugural address—Jefferson indicated a willingness to cooperate with members of the opposition party. "We are all Republicans—we are all Federalists," he said. Soon, though, under a certain amount of pressure from members of his party, Jefferson's position began to shift. Initially uncertain about whether to remove all or none of the Federalists in office, he gradually decided to ensure that his fellow Republicans held about two-thirds of all political jobs. Federalists were removed from office and replaced with Republicans to achieve this balance. Those appointed at the last minute by Adams were the first to go.

Jefferson's party was noteworthy for its organization. This depended, in large part, on the Republican members of Congress, who supplied the party's leadership in Congress and also, through connections in their home states, helped maintain a consistent message for local and state organizations.

Washington, D.C., was a new capital—and a new city—when Jefferson became president, and few congressmen had homes there. Instead, they lived and ate together in boardinghouses. Over breakfasts and dinners, they had heated discussions and hammered out the key issues of the day. The representatives tended to socialize with members of their own party—taverns and boardinghouses tended to attract either Republican or Federalist customers, but seldom both.

VICE PRESIDENT

For the election of 1804, it was clear that Thomas Jefferson would once more be his party's nominee for president.

Leaders of the Republican Party decided to focus on their nominee for vice president.

The Twelfth Amendment had not yet been ratified (although it ultimately would be ratified before the election), so there was not yet a system in place for nominating both president and vice president on a single ballot. Instead, the old system still was in use. Whoever received the most electoral votes would become president; the runner-up would

JEFFERSON'S FIRST INAUGURAL ADDRESS

On March 4, 1801, Thomas Jefferson became the first president inaugurated in the new capital of Washington, D.C. In his inaugural address, he spoke of the bitter campaign that had preceded the election:

> . . . We have called by different names brethren of the same principle. We are all Republicans, we are all Federalists. . . . Let us then, with courage and confidence pursue our own Federal and Republican principles, our attachment to union and representative government. Kindly separated by nature and a wide ocean from the exterminating havoc of one quarter of the globe; too high-minded to endure the degradations of the others; possessing a chosen country, with room enough for our descendants to the thousandth and thousandth generation; entertaining a due sense of our equal right to the use of our own faculties, to the acquisitions of our own industry, to honor and confidence from our fellow-citizens, resulting not from birth, but from our actions and their

be vice president. Republicans wanted to select a potential vice president who was popular and appealing enough to surpass all other candidates but not so strong that he would get more votes than Jefferson.

Aaron Burr, Jefferson's vice president in his first term, was not considered for the ticket this time. Burr and Jefferson had initially tied in the election of 1800, and Jefferson had always questioned Burr's loyalty and largely ignored

sense of them; enlightened by a benign religion, professed, indeed, and practiced in various forms, yet all of them inculcating honesty, truth, temperance, gratitude, and the love of man; acknowledging and adoring an overruling Providence, which by all its dispensations proves that it delights in the happiness of man here and his greater happiness hereafter—with all these blessings, what more is necessary to make us a happy and a prosperous people? Still one thing more, fellow-citizens—a wise and frugal Government, which shall restrain men from injuring one another, shall leave them otherwise free to regulate their own pursuits of industry and improvement, and shall not take from the mouth of labor the bread it has earned. This is the sum of good government. . . .

Source: "Thomas Jefferson First Inaugural Address." The Avalon Project at Yale Law School. Available online. URL: http://www.yale.edu/lawweb/avalon/presiden /inaug/jefinau1.htm. Updated on March 4, 2007.

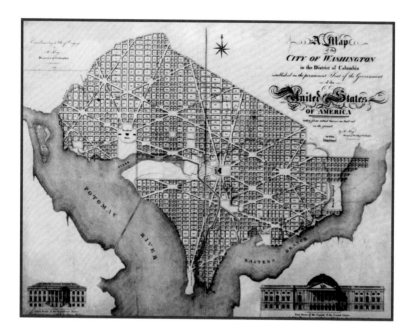

Thomas Jefferson was the first president to be inaugurated in Washington, D.C. Above is a map of the city as it looked in the early 1800s.

him during the first term. While serving as vice president, Burr ran for election as governor of New York but was defeated. Later, he was involved in a duel with Alexander Hamilton that resulted in Hamilton's death.

In February 1804, a group of Republicans gathered and nominated a committee of men whose goal was to "promote the success of the Republican nominations." Thirteen men were chosen for the committee: Seven were senators, six were members of the House of Representatives, and they were from 13 different states. Their mission was not only to ensure Thomas Jefferson's reelection but also to guarantee that his vice president was a supportive Republican.

This was a significant development in party politics, as this group of 13 men represents the first formal national party organization established to elect a president and vice president. The party's ultimate choice for the vice presidential candidate was the governor of New York, George Clinton. In addition to his experience and political prominence, Clinton added geographical balance to a ticket whose presidential candidate came from Virginia.

The party was particularly eager to focus its attention on the New England states. Before 1800, New England had been strongly Federalist. During Jefferson's presidency, his party concentrated its efforts on ensuring that the Republican Party was not merely a Southern political party, but a national party.

Party organizations were set up in each state. By October 1801, instructions had been given out to party organizers in each town. These party committees were told to make up a list of all those eligible to vote in their towns, especially those likely to consider themselves Republican. The committees were told to hold a private meeting of these Republicans and to discuss with them the importance of ensuring that Republican principles were maintained in local government. The committees were also told to try to make sure that Republican newspapers were circulated in their towns. These early organizations formed the basis of party structure at the local level.

In 1804, when Jefferson sought reelection, his party re-minded voters of the failures of Federalist president John Adams and provided a list of Jefferson's accomplishments during his four years in office. These included reduction of taxes, elimination of several thousand unnecessary government jobs, reduction of the national debt, mainte-nance of peace, and the purchase of the Louisiana terri-tory. It is interesting to note that, apart from the Louisiana Purchase, many similar claims feature in modern presi-dential campaigns.

Adams and the Federalists were also linked—unfavorably—to Great Britain. The Revolutionary War was still recent history, and voters were reminded that Great Britain had been America's greatest enemy not long ago. Federalists responded by linking their party to George Washington. They organized a large public celebration of George Washington's birthday and de-scribed a vote for the Federalist candidates as a vote for the "Washington ticket."

In the end, Jefferson was overwhelmingly successful in his bid for reelection. He won every state except Delaware and Connecticut.

JEFFERSON'S SUCCESSOR

There was pressure on Jefferson to run for a third term as president when the election of 1808 drew closer. He was the clear leader of his party: Its goals had been shaped by his vision for the country.

Jefferson's second term had not been as smooth or peaceful as his first term, however, and there was growing conflict with Great Britain. Jefferson believed that the country was now set on a course that would ensure its long-term success. He wanted to spend his remaining years at his home in Virginia.

Three men vied for the Republican nomination once it became clear that Jefferson would not run for a third term: Secretary of State James Madison, Vice President George Clinton, and James Monroe. Some people used this competition to try to persuade Jefferson to change his mind. They wanted him to seek a third term in order to prevent a split in the party he had founded. Jefferson held firm, though, and made it clear that Madison was his choice as a successor. Ultimately, George Clinton was nominated by the party as Madison's running mate.

Madison faced the same Federalist candidate who had challenged Thomas Jefferson in 1804: Charles Pinckney of South Carolina. Jefferson's party again triumphed. Madison won 122 electoral votes to Pinckney's 44. The party had held the presidency for eight years and ensured its transition to a new president. It was a clear demonstration that the values and positions of the party mattered as much to the voters as did the personal appeal of Thomas Jefferson. It was also a demonstration of the party's success at transmitting its message to the voters.

MADISON IN OFFICE

Much of the Republican Party's early success had been based on the leadership offered by members of Congress; however, the split that had resulted in three different men

In 1808, James Madison, the Republican candidate for president, won 122 electoral votes and the presidency. He was the nation's fourth president and was elected to two terms.

vying for the presidency reflected a split in the Republican congressional leadership, as well. Each candidate had his own backers in Congress, and the supporters of Monroe and Clinton were less willing to work with Madison because he was not "their" candidate.

For this reason, Madison began his presidency facing greater challenges than those Jefferson had encountered during his first months in office. Madison was aware of the importance of ensuring support from Congress, and as a result he tried to please various factions by appointing their nominees to governmental positions, regardless of their skills or abilities.

Jefferson had clearly been the party leader during his presidency. Under Madison, leadership of the party seemed more firmly held by Congress members. Conflict with Great Britain soon made it clear that war was likely; the Federalists pounced on this, proclaiming themselves to be the "party of peace," whereas Madison's Republicans were described as the "war party."

American forces were not adequately prepared for the War of 1812. In the mid-term elections, many of the older Republicans in Congress had been replaced by new, younger candidates. These younger congressmen had not experienced the Revolutionary War firsthand, so the America they knew was very different from that of men like Jefferson and Madison. Many of them were Southerners and Westerners, and they elected Henry Clay of Kentucky as Speaker of the House. Their focus was on expanding American territory. They had not lived through a war with Great Britain, and as a result, their expectations for the war were optimistic, even unrealistic. Thus, Congress did not act quickly when it came to building up the American Navy or raising taxes to provide funds for the military campaign.

The likelihood that Madison would lead the country into war created a split within the party and the country as the presidential election of 1812 drew close. A vote for Madison equaled, in the minds of some voters, a vote for war with England. A group of Republicans from New York broke away from the party and nominated DeWitt Clinton as their candidate for president. Clinton won all of the New England states, with one exception—Vermont—and all of the Middle Atlantic states except Pennsylvania. Madison won by only 39 electoral votes, scarcely an endorsement for his policies or his presidency.

The Republicans benefited from a weak Federalist Party; otherwise Madison might not have been re-elected. Still, the party faced internal schisms: a split between Republicans of different ages and from different regions of the country and a split between those who favored war and those who favored peace. The definitions that had once separated the nation into Republicans and Federalists were no longer clear, replaced instead by other definitions of how the future of the country should be shaped.

AMERICA AT WAR

In 1814, the British launched attacks in New York and in New Orleans. The British attacked cities along the Atlantic coast, and by August, British ships were sailing up the Potomac River to Washington, D.C., where they burned

The Battle of New Orleans, depicted in the illustration above, contributed to Andrew Jackson's reputation as a war hero. He led troops made up of volunteers, free blacks, slaves, and French pirates to defeat the British.

the White House and the Capitol. President Madison was forced to flee to Virginia. It was a humiliation for the president—but one that served to rally the nation behind the war effort.

One of the most significant battles in the war was fought in New Orleans, where General Andrew Jackson defeated the British with a force made up of volunteers, slaves, free blacks, and about 1,000 French pirates. The battle would prove to be one of the most decisive of the war, and Jackson's triumphs would make him a war hero and later an important political figure.

There was one last internal challenge that Madison needed to settle while the war was still being fought. Several New England states (including Vermont, Massachusetts, Rhode Island, and Connecticut) were dissatisfied with Madison's leadership. They decided to protest the war, debated secession (separating from the rest of the United States), and chose to negotiate a separate peace with England. They sent representatives to Washington, D.C., to present their demands. When the representatives arrived, they learned of Jackson's defeat of the British at New Orleans and that a peace treaty had been signed in Belgium. Madison could have publicly humiliated the states for their disloyalty, but instead he allowed the representatives to quietly return home. Nevertheless, the action was perceived to be a Federalist effort and contributed to a further decline of the Federalist Party.

JAMES MONROE

As Madison's second term in office came to an end, the Republican nominating committee chose James Monroe as Madison's successor. Daniel Tompkins, the former governor of New York, was chosen as his running mate. Some Republicans grumbled about a "Virginia dynasty"—like Madison and Jefferson, Monroe was a Virginia native—but the only serious challenger Monroe faced for the Republican nomination was another Southerner, William Crawford, who had also been born in Virginia. The Republicans had hit on a winning formula: a presidential candidate from Virginia whose running mate was a former governor of New York. Monroe easily won election over his Federalist challenger, Rufus King of New York, who made no effort to campaign and won only 3 states (Massachusetts, Connecticut, and Delaware) to Monroe's 16.

The ease with which Monroe had won election and the general disarray of the Federalists seemed to suggest that America would evolve into a single-party nation—or perhaps a nation with no political parties at all. Andrew Jackson, serving as commander of the federal army in the South, suggested to Monroe that he bring an end to the party system by ignoring party affiliation when choosing his cabinet. Monroe was not yet willing to do so; however, he did choose John Quincy Adams, son of the last Federalist president, to serve as his secretary of state.

Monroe began his presidency with a tour of the states; he was the first president to do so since George Washington. His tour prompted such a favorable response from the people, who relished the opportunity to see their president, that the early years of his presidency were soon being described as the "Era of Good Feelings." The country continued to expand to the south and west, and four new states—Alabama, Illinois, Indiana, and Mississippi—joined the Union.

Most Americans were still farmers, although industry was growing, particularly in the Northeast. Monroe traveled to the West several times, and during his presidency the western boundary of the United States was set at the Pacific Ocean. In addition, the territory of Florida was granted to the United States in a treaty with Spain.

Slavery was gradually becoming the focus of more intense political debates. It was an issue that would deeply affect Monroe's party—the party that would eventually become the Democratic Party. Under Monroe's presidency, the issue that would transform the Union first began to divide North and South.

3

A PARTY DIVIDED

In 1819, the Missouri Territory petitioned to join the Union as a state. At the time, America was evenly split into states that did permit slavery and those that did not, with 11 on each side. The Constitution had stated that the issue of whether or not to allow slavery was up to each individual state. Republican Congressman James Talmadge of New York, however, suggested that Missouri's petition to join the Union contain an amendment stating that no additional slaves could be brought into the state and that those that were already there would eventually be set free.

This proposal launched a fierce debate in Congress. Southern congressmen argued that each state had the right to decide whether or not to permit slavery. The debate was finally resolved with a compromise in March 1820. Missouri could join the United States as a slave

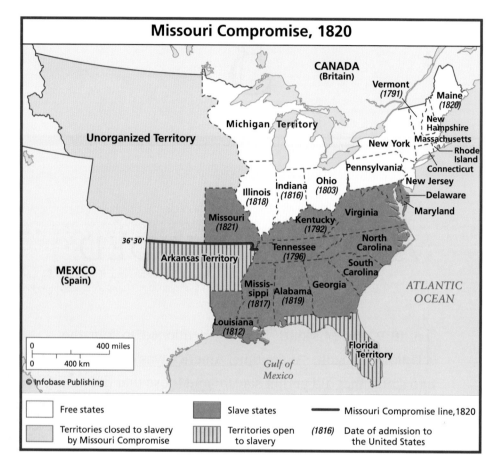

Missouri Compromise, 1820

CANADA
(Britain)

Vermont
(1791)

Maine
(1820)

New
Hampshire

Michigan Territory

New York   Massachusetts

Unorganized Territory

Rhode
Island

Pennsylvania   Connecticut

Illinois   Indiana   Ohio   New Jersey
(1818)   (1816)   (1803)

Delaware

Missouri   Virginia   Maryland
(1821)

Kentucky
(1792)

36°30'

North
Carolina

Tennessee
(1796)

Arkansas Territory

MEXICO
(Spain)

South
Carolina

Missis-   Georgia
sippi   Alabama
(1817)   (1819)

ATLANTIC
OCEAN

Louisiana
(1812)

Florida
Territory

0   400 miles

0   400 km

© Infobase Publishing

Gulf of
Mexico

	Free states		Slave states		Missouri Compromise line, 1820
	Territories closed to slavery by Missouri Compromise		Territories open to slavery	(1816)	Date of admission to the United States

When the Missouri Territory petitioned to join the United States, the nation was evenly split between states that permitted slavery and those that did not. The Missouri Compromise of 1820 allowed Missouri in as a slave state while Maine joined the Union as a free state.

state, but Maine would also join as a free state. Additional laws were passed to ban slavery in all remaining territory acquired in the Louisiana Purchase, north of a specific line of latitude. Many political figures—including

John Quincy Adams and Thomas Jefferson—saw the Missouri Compromise as a dangerous sign of division within the United States, where lines that separated slave states from free states were drawn.

Today, the Missouri Compromise is viewed as a political mistake. In 1820, however, as Monroe sought reelection, his administration's policies were viewed favorably—so favorably, in fact, that the Republican members of Congress felt that it was not necessary to discuss nominations: Monroe was the clear choice. The Federalists were unable to mount any kind of real challenge. America had become essentially a one-party country, and that one party was the Democratic-Republican Party. Monroe received all but one of the Electoral College votes; that single vote went to John Quincy Adams. It is interesting to note that President John Adams, John Quincy's father and a member of the Electoral College, was not responsible for casting that single vote. He voted for Monroe.

In Monroe's second term, he developed the foreign policy position that would become a defining achievement in America's role in global affairs. Known as the Monroe Doctrine, the policy was created in response to Monroe's effort to support the independence recently declared by former Spanish and Portuguese colonies in Latin America. Monroe was determined not only to support the independence of these nations but also to firmly state to the European powers that the United States would oppose any further attempt to colonize lands in the Western Hemisphere.

This significant achievement took place during Monroe's second term, but the end of his presidency was also beset by confusion within his party. Power to nominate presidential candidates had been held firmly by congressional Republicans, but their power was slipping away as

THE ELECTORAL COLLEGE

Presidents are elected based not on the number of popular votes they receive, but on the number of Electoral College votes. Each state has a certain number of electors (representatives to the Electoral College) who cast votes for that state. The number is based on the number of senators from the state (always two) and the number of U.S. representatives (which varies from state to state based on population).

In the presidential election, the party whose candidate has won the most popular votes in a state wins all the electors of that state. The exceptions to this are Maine and Nebraska—two electors are chosen by statewide popular vote and the remainder are chosen by the popular vote within each congressional district.

Because certain states have more congressional representatives, these states have more electors. Presidential campaigns often focus on states with the most electoral votes—California is the largest, with 55. Other key states include Texas (34), New York (31), Florida (27), Pennsylvania and Illinois (21 each), and Ohio (20). The candidate for president with the most electoral votes (it must be at least one more than half of the total) is declared president.

state legislatures assumed a greater role in party politics. In addition, with more and more eligible voters—that is, white males—the focus of the party shifted toward appealing to those voters in a more direct way.

A DIVISIVE ELECTION

Campaigning for the election of 1824 began two years earlier, as various candidates began to position themselves to receive their parties' nominations. At one point, there were as many as 16 potential candidates for the Republican Party's nomination. Gradually, they were whittled down to 6 and then to 4: Secretary of State John Quincy Adams, the former Federalist from Massachusetts; William Crawford, the secretary of the treasury; Henry Clay, the Speaker of the House of Representatives; and Andrew Jackson, the military hero who had been elected as a senator from Tennessee.

The party that had been so disciplined in bringing Thomas Jefferson, James Madison, and James Monroe to office had lost its focus. Chaos reigned as competing interests lobbied for their candidates.

Without party organization supporting a particular candidate, the election proved to be a mess. Voter turnout was very low, little more than 25 percent. Andrew Jackson led in both the electoral and popular votes, but by such a small number that he failed to achieve the necessary majority of electoral votes. This meant that the election had to be decided in the House of Representatives. According to the Constitution, only the leading three candidates were to be considered. Clay had received the fewest electoral votes, so he was eliminated. Crawford was suffering from a serious illness, misdiagnosed as a stroke, so he, too, was not considered in the House. The contest came down to John Quincy Adams and Andrew Jackson.

Clay was soon the focus of intense lobbying efforts by backers of Adams and Jackson, who wanted his support for their candidates. Clay did not like Jackson, however, and did not think that he had the qualifications to serve as president. Clay met several times with Adams and ultimately gave his support (and his electoral votes) to Adams, who was then declared to be president. Jackson and his supporters were outraged and declared that some sort of secret deal had been made to steal the election from the man who had received the most votes. Their suspicions seemed to be proved correct when, shortly after Adams was elected, he appointed Clay to serve as his secretary of state.

This difficult beginning marked much of John Quincy Adams's presidency. His credibility damaged by the suggestion that the election had not been fairly won, Adams found it difficult to work with Congress. His party—his adopted party, since he had once been a Federalist—had been hurt by the election and split into various groups. Many congressmen were outspoken in their criticism of Adams; Martin Van Buren, a senator from New York, and John Randolph, a senator from Virginia, were among the worst. In fact, Randolph was so outspoken in his criticism of the Adams administration, and Secretary of State Clay in particular, that Clay eventually challenged Randolph

The sixth president of the United States, John Quincy Adams (above), was the son of the second president, John Adams. Quincy Adams had a difficult presidency; in particular, he found it hard to work with Congress.

to a duel. The senator and secretary of state fired at each other, but Randolph's cloak received the only damage from this exchange of gunfire.

Adams's presidency was marked by such intense disagreement among members of his own party that his
single term in office can be viewed today as the end of
an era. The Republican Party that had produced four
presidents would forever be changed in the years that
followed; it would be divided in two. Supporters of Clay
and older members of the party renamed themselves
National Republicans. Andrew Jackson led the other
group that split from the party. That group was known
as the Democratic Party, the name by which the party is
known today.

THE PARTY OF THE PEOPLE

The party founded by Thomas Jefferson had first come
into power claiming itself as the "party of the people." The
presidents who had been elected by this party, however,
owed perhaps less to the people than to a select group
of men: the congressional Republican caucus (nominating committee). Jefferson, Monroe, and Madison represented a distinct type—Virginians and well-educated,
wealthy men who had played a role in America since
its founding. With Madison, Monroe, and even Adams,
a standard had been set. A politician would spend a
certain amount of time serving in a president's cabinet
and then essentially be selected by that president as
his successor.

With the election of Andrew Jackson in 1828, the party—
and the presidency—entered a new phase. For one thing,
voters played a greater role than ever before in ensuring

the election of Jackson. Gradually, since 1810, the voting policies in states had been changing. In the oldest states, voting had been restricted to those who owned property of some sort or paid taxes. As new states joined the Union, this began to change, and gradually one state after another began to shift its voting policies so that the right to vote was given to all white males over the age of 21.

This was an incredibly important shift. Once, presidents had been chosen based on connections and political influence, but suddenly a candidate could appeal directly to the voters and voters could use their influence to select the candidate who most appealed to them. In 1828, Andrew Jackson was that candidate. The brash war hero was tremendously popular, and many viewed the election of 1824 as having been "stolen" from him.

Gradually, the split in the Republican Party had begun to emerge. Martin Van Buren perhaps first contributed to the split, although he did so to advance his candidate (Jackson). In 1827, he gathered a committee of men in Nashville whose aim was to communicate with other "Jackson committees" in other parts of the country.

At the time, candidates for the presidency did not actively campaign for office—it was not regarded as dignified. The campaigning was left to their supporters, and Van Buren was more than willing to campaign actively on Jackson's behalf. Jackson certainly presented a more colorful image than Adams. In addition to his reputation as a military hero, Jackson proudly described himself as a rough "backwoodsman." Jackson's nickname, "Old Hickory," became

the basis for a whole campaign. Hickory Clubs were organized, and hickory trees were planted at political rallies.
Political souvenirs such as plates, pitchers, and ladies' hair
combs were all stamped with pictures of Jackson.

The contest between Adams and Jackson was described
by Jackson supporters as a contest between democracy
and aristocracy—Jackson, of course, represented the side
of democracy. Newspapers that supported one side or the
other published gossip and rumors about both men.

Jackson's campaign as a "common man" proved victori-
ous, with especially strong support in the South and West.
Adams took New England, but Jackson won nearly every
other state except Delaware, Maryland, and New Jersey.

PRESIDENT JACKSON

Jackson entered the presidency with little political experience; he had been elected in large part because of his
military career, rather than his career as a senator. It is
important to note that, although he was the first American
president raised in humble circumstances, he was not poor
when elected to office. He cultivated his image as a back-
woods man and frontiersman, but Jackson had established
a successful career and achieved great wealth in his life-
time—he had built a fortune speculating in land. His home
was a mansion near Nashville, and he owned slaves.

Jackson created for his party what came to be known as
"Jacksonian Democracy," a philosophy that had much in
common with Jefferson's idealized vision of an America of
hardworking farmers and planters. Jackson's presidential

policies would reflect this preference for agriculture as the most important occupation and his disregard for the wealthy. Under Jackson, federal jobs were deliberately handed out to those who shared his political views.

When Jackson sought reelection in 1832, the split between members of his party was complete. The more traditional wing of the party labeled itself the National Republicans. Jackson and his supporters wanted to clearly distinguish themselves from this group. They took the name "Democratic Party" to demonstrate their connection to the concept of democracy.

The first national conventions were held for this election. The National Republicans held their convention in December 1831. Their nominee for the presidency was Henry Clay. Five months later, 334 Democrats met in Baltimore. They represented every state except Missouri, and their unanimous choice was Jackson, with Martin Van Buren as his running mate.

This convention was an important milestone for the Democratic Party. Procedures were set up for future conventions and future nominations, ensuring that this was not Jackson's party, but a party that would endure beyond a single election or a single candidate. Majority rule dictated which candidate would be chosen. Two-thirds of the delegates needed to approve not only the presidential but also the vice-presidential nominee.

Jackson easily won reelection, and the Democratic Party was established not as a branch of the Republican Party but as a political party in its own right. Thanks to Jackson, it was identified as the party of the common man; the wealthy and the elite were labeled its opponents. The Democratic Party still retains some of this image today.

In his second term, Jackson challenged the national bank system, shifting federal money from the national bank to a series of state banks. The banking issue prompted a group of businessmen and opponents of Jackson's to band together in an effort to oppose the man they labeled "King Andrew I." They called themselves "Whigs," after the British political party formed to oppose the king of England in the 1700s. Soon, they would develop into a political force, particularly in New England.

Jackson's presidency was marked by prosperity, but his economic policies would prove problematic for his successor. Jackson disliked paper money and insisted that, when public lands were sold, payment could be made only with gold or silver.

It was also under Jackson that many Native Americans were forcibly moved from their native lands in Georgia to the so-called "Indian Territory" in the west. The aim was to open up Southern land for cotton planting. The Supreme Court tried to protect the Native Americans, but Jackson defied the court and ordered federal troops to escort the tribes to the west.

MARTIN VAN BUREN

In 1836, the Democrats again gathered in Baltimore. Vice President Martin Van Buren, the man who had masterminded Jackson's campaign, was the party's choice for president. Richard Mentor Johnson of Kentucky was Jackson's choice for vice president, and the party followed his wishes.

Van Buren was the son of a tavernkeeper from the small village of Kinderhook, New York. He had become a leader in New York state politics in what was then the Republican Party, and although eventually elected senator, he remained in close touch with his state organization. Van Buren understood the importance of an organized, disciplined state party, and he had helped develop this organization as the Democratic Party was formed.

Van Buren had put his full effort into ensuring Jackson's election, and Jackson returned the favor by campaigning for Van Buren. Van Buren was an experienced politician—far more experienced than Jackson had been—and he believed deeply in the Democratic Party. He felt that the Democratic Party's principles, low taxes, no national debt, states' rights, and strict interpretation of the Constitution, should be clearly expressed to voters.

Van Buren's hope was that the party's convention would focus on these ideas. Instead, the convention's message to voters—the type of message that would eventually be known as the party's platform—focused on party heroes like Jefferson, Madison, Monroe, and Jackson. Van Buren, the actual nominee, was mentioned only once.

Despite Jackson's support for his candidacy and the backing of the organized Democratic Party structure, Van Buren barely won the popular vote, earning 50.9 percent.

He did, however, receive a majority of the electoral votes and assumed the presidency in 1837.

The Democratic Party had been shaped by Van Buren but was transformed by events in the nation and by Jackson's appeal to voters. Whereas once congressional caucuses had played a key role in choosing the candidate, the national convention had assumed that function, and not only national but also local and state politicians now played an important role in party politics.

Under Jackson, the Democratic Party had become, in a sense, a party that had achieved success because of the president's willingness to divide Americans. Jackson drew a distinction between the wealthy and the poor, the laborers and the business owners, and even divided Southerners and Westerners from those in the East.

Jackson's legacy was a challenging one for Van Buren who, though a seasoned politician, had none of Jackson's charisma. Van Buren was further burdened by the legacy of Jackson's economic policies. Only weeks after Van Buren took office, New York banks began to cut back on loans in an effort to bring a halt to widespread speculation. Soon, banks across the country followed suit and a panic resulted in the worst depression the nation had known. Banks and businesses closed down, and unemployment rose to record levels. Van Buren insisted on following Jackson's policies of accepting only hard currency (gold and silver) rather than paper money, refusing to charter a national bank, and taking few steps that could stem the crisis.

The Whig Party was quick to seize on the opportunity offered by the financial crisis. They labeled the president "Martin Van Ruin" and selected William Henry Harrison as their candidate in the 1840 presidential campaign. The Whigs skillfully presented Harrison as a candidate similar to Jackson—a military hero who had defeated the British at the Battle of the Thames. Harrison was given the nickname "Old Tippecanoe" and was presented as another self-made candidate of humble beginnings, with images of a log cabin often appearing on posters that advertised his candidacy. There was little truth in this political image making. Harrison was the son of an aristocratic Virginia family and had lived on an impressive estate in the Ohio countryside. In fact, Van Buren's childhood had been far humbler than Harrison's. Nonetheless, Van Buren was depicted by the Whigs as a polished, elegantly dressed politician and contrasted with their candidate who, they claimed, liked nothing more than a swig of hard cider from a jug. Campaign speakers suggested to voters that the choice was "between the log cabin and the palace, between hard cider and champagne." Harrison's running mate was John Tyler of Virginia, who had been a Democrat but left the party after disagreeing with many of Jackson's policies.

The Democratic convention was held in Baltimore in May 1840. It was at this convention that the party's name was officially changed from Democratic-Republican Party to Democratic Party. The party nominated Van Buren but did not name a vice-presidential candidate.

The Whigs proved their mastery of the campaign, using the symbols of the log cabin and cider jugs to promote their candidate and transform the election into entertainment. Nearly 80 percent of all those eligible to vote did so in the election. Van Buren lost. The era of Jacksonian democracy had come to an end.

4

SLAVERY AND THE DEMOCRATIC PARTY

By the middle of the nineteenth century, slavery was emerging as an issue of increasing political focus. The question about whether or not slavery should be permitted was nothing new to political debate, but, by the mid-1800s more and more focus was placed on how to respond to slavery.

For the election of 1840, in which Martin Van Buren was defeated in his bid for reelection, a group of abolitionists (activists who attempted to have slavery outlawed) formed their own political party—the Liberty Party—and nominated their own candidate for president. Although their bid for the presidency was unsuccessful, it was a sign that slavery was becoming an issue that presidential candidates would need to address. That issue would prove particularly disastrous for the Democratic Party.

From 1841 to 1845, the Whigs occupied the White House. William Henry Harrison served as president for only a month before dying of pneumonia. He was the first president to die in office. John Tyler, the vice president, became president. The former Democrat struggled to work with the Whig Congress members; their disgust with his policies became so strong that the Whigs ultimately decided to expel Tyler from their party. An impeachment resolution was introduced in the House of Representatives, but it failed to pass.

When the Democratic convention was again held in Baltimore, President Tyler sent representatives to suggest that he should be nominated by the Democrats. Martin Van Buren also sought the nomination, but his outspoken position on whether or not Texas should be annexed (forcibly added) by the United States (he was opposed, fearing that it would spark a war with Mexico) caused him to lose the support of most delegates.

It took several ballots before a frontrunner emerged, and that frontrunner was a man who had come to the convention hoping to be nominated as vice president. James K. Polk had served as Speaker of the House of Representatives and governor of Tennessee, yet he was essentially a little-known candidate—so little known, in fact, that the Whig campaign repeatedly posed the question, "Who is James K. Polk?"

James K. Polk *(shown here)* was the Democratic candidate for president in 1844. Although he was essentially unknown before he began campaigning, he gained the support of Andrew Jackson, which helped him win the election.

Polk, though, sensing that most Americans wanted to see their country expand, spoke out in favor of annexing Texas and Oregon, and he had the support of the aging Andrew Jackson. Expansion became his issue, and this emphasis was popular in the South and the West. Slavery existed in the background of this issue: Texas's entry into the United States would tip the balance in favor of slave-holding states. Polk's tough stance against Mexico (which claimed Texas) and Great Britain (which claimed portions of Oregon) was also popular. He won the election and, shortly after his victory, Congress voted to annex Texas.

Polk kept to his promise of expanding the country. He signed a treaty with the British that brought Oregon in as American territory. Disputes over territory were followed by war with Mexico, but American forces were successful. In the end, Polk added not only Texas but also New Mexico and California to American territory. With this new territory, however, came the question that had haunted each American effort to expand: Would slavery be allowed in these new territories?

LINES OF DIVISION

Polk himself was a slave owner. His belief was that, since cotton could not grow in the soil of the American west, slavery would probably never develop there. He suggested that California be introduced into the Union as a free state to balance the slave state of Texas.

The question of slavery was moving beyond the idea of balance, however, to a broader moral question: Should the United States be a nation that allowed human beings to live in bondage? Northern Democrats were increasingly outspoken in their efforts to ensure that slavery was banned in any new territory acquired by the United States. This triggered a split with Southern Democrats, also known as "Dixie Democrats," who felt that the party was losing touch with Southern interests.

Polk had stated that, when elected, he would serve only one term. The split in the party made the choice of the party's next candidate for the presidency particularly critical.

At the 1848 convention, an antislavery group wanted to nominate Martin Van Buren. A proslavery group wanted to nominate John C. Calhoun, who had formed a Southern Rights Movement to pressure the Democratic Party and had stated that his delegates would never support a candidate who took a position against slavery. Finally, a third group, which supported Lewis Cass, favored allowing the territories to decide for themselves whether or not to permit slavery. Cass was chosen almost as a compromise candidate, in an effort to avoid alienating supporters on either end of the slavery issue. The effort would fail.

Despite the bitterness and chaos, the 1848 Democratic convention is noteworthy because at this convention, the decision was made to establish a formal Democratic National Committee, with one member for each state. It was decided that the committee would meet during congressional and presidential election years to plan and coordinate strategy.

Above is a campaign banner for the Free Soil Party candidates in 1848, Martin Van Buren and Charles Adams. Van Buren and his supporters left the Democratic Party after the party nominated a compromise candidate for that year's election.

The choice of Cass, intended as a compromise, ultimately pleased few Democrats. Van Buren and his supporters criticized their party as a "Slavocracy" and left, forming their own party in Buffalo, which they called the Free Soil Party. Their platform consisted of opposition to slavery in any form in the new territories. The Free Soilers were joined by many former Whigs when that party nominated General Zachary Taylor, a hero of the Mexican War who was himself a slave owner in Louisiana.

THE 1850 COMPROMISE

In an effort to address the question of whether or not slavery should be permitted in newly acquired U.S. territories, President Millard Fillmore championed what became known as the 1850 Compromise. The following points were presented to the Senate as five separate bills:

1. Admit California as a free state.
2. Settle the Texas boundary by allowing New Mexico to keep most of its land and compensating Texas for the areas it had claimed.
3. Grant territorial status to New Mexico.
4. Place federal officers at the disposal of slaveholders seeking fugitive slaves.
5. Outlaw the slave trade in the District of Columbia.

Each of the bills passed, and, on September 20, 1850, President Fillmore signed them into law. Although intended as a way to preserve the Union, they would only temporarily keep the peace between the North and the South.

Taylor was an unusual choice for the Whigs. He was not a Whig—in fact, he claimed that he belonged to no political party. He also stated that he had never voted in a presidential election.

Nevertheless, the Free Soilers managed to pull enough votes away from the Democratic candidate, Cass, to ultimately result in the election of Taylor in the first presidential election in which all states voted on the same day. Pro- and antislavery supporters within the Democratic Party saw the election results as evidence that their position was the correct one. The party could not afford to compromise, but would need to resolve its position on slavery once and for all.

COMPROMISE

Taylor's solution to the slaveholding crisis was to have the new territories quickly become states. They would then vote on whether or not to permit slavery. When Southern leaders threatened that their states would leave the Union, Taylor boldly faced them down, promising to lead the army against them and hang anyone found guilty of rebelling against the Union. Taylor collapsed after participating in a ceremony on a particularly hot July 4, however, and died a few days later. His successor, Millard Fillmore, was also a supporter of this compromise effort—but Fillmore had signed the controversial Fugitive Slave Act, which allowed slave owners to hunt down slaves who had fled to free states, capture them, and take them back into slavery.

Gathering for its convention in Baltimore in 1852, the Democratic Party vowed to resist any efforts to readdress the question of slavery in or out of Congress. Their nominee was Franklin Pierce, a former senator from New Hampshire, who had served as a general in the Mexican War and refused to take a strong position on the slavery issue. He was elected in part because the Democrats' support for the 1850 Compromise was more clearly expressed, and many voters believed that the Compromise would ensure peace.

Pierce entered office benefiting from a general prosperity and a boom in railroading that would soon unite the two coasts; however, he was forced to deal with the consequences of a disastrous action taken by a member of his own party. Stephen Douglas, a senator from Illinois, helped draft and then force through a bill known as the Kansas-Nebraska Act. Douglas supported the building of a railroad from Chicago to California. In an effort to organize the Western territories through which the railroad would pass, Douglas's bill proposed that the residents of these territories would decide the question of whether or not slavery would be allowed, essentially repealing the Missouri Compromise. As a result, anti- and proslavery settlers rushed into Kansas and violence followed.

Despite public outcry, Pierce signed the Kansas-Nebraska Act, further propelling the nation toward the Civil War. Many Democrats, disgusted by this action, left the party. Some, who claimed to be the ones who truly believed in Jefferson's principles of individual freedom,

Franklin Pierce was the Democratic candidate for the election of 1852. He won by a landslide, 254 electoral votes to 42, against the Whig party candidate.

helped to launch a new party, one that they called "Republican" in honor of Jefferson's original party. This group formed the roots of what would become the modern Republican Party.

For their 1856 convention, the Democrats gathered in Cincinnati. The platform endorsed the Kansas-Nebraska

Act as a "sound and safe solution of the 'slavery question,'" but Pierce was not renominated. The party instead turned to James Buchanan, who had served as Pierce's minister to Great Britain. His time out of the country contributed to his appeal. He had not been in the United States and so had not been involved in some of the most hostile fights of the past few years.

Buchanan's philosophy was that the decision about slavery belonged to the Constitution and to the Supreme Court. The bitterness over slavery had become too great for either side to accept a policy that favored the opposing position, however. Buchanan further added to the crisis when he suggested that Kansas be admitted to the Union as a slave state, angering Northerners, members of his own party, and the newly formed Republican Party. Kansas remained a territory, and Republicans gained a majority in the House in the midterm elections of 1858. Northern and Southern senators argued over bills. The country was dividing, and Buchanan lacked the skill or understanding to hold it together. He could not, in fact, even hold his own party together.

A DIVIDED CONVENTION

In April 1860, the Democratic convention was held in Charleston, South Carolina, a friendly gesture toward the South to prevent the party from splitting. The gesture would prove unsuccessful. The Northern Democrats pushed hard for Stephen Douglas as their candidate. A group of Southern Democrats declared that they would leave the party unless its platform promised to guarantee slavery in the American territories. Douglas and his supporters bitterly opposed this, insisting instead that the subject of slavery should be voted on in each of the territories.

When the Southern Democrats failed to obtain the promise they wanted, many of them (including the entire delegation from Alabama) walked out of the convention. Douglas failed to gather the majority he needed, and the decision was made to hold a second convention in Baltimore.

The Baltimore meeting was every bit as disastrous as the one in Charleston. The acrimony between delegates from the North and the South continued. As a particularly bad omen, the floor of the convention hall collapsed during the meeting, forcing delegates to rush from the hall and stay away until the floor could be repaired. Douglas supporters refused to allow the delegates from Alabama and Louisiana (many of whom had walked out on the earlier meeting) to participate in the new meeting, prompting yet another walkout by delegates from many Southern states, including Virginia, as well as those from California and Oregon. When the meeting finally ended, Douglas was chosen as the nominee.

The battle was not yet over. The Southern Democrats who had walked out at the meeting held their own convention in Charleston. They took the name "National Democrats" and chose as their nominee Vice President John Breckinridge of Kentucky, with Senator Joseph Lane as his running mate. Their platform focused on protecting slavery. With the Democratic Party running two separate candidates and essentially two separate campaigns—one in the North and one in the South—it is not surprising that the newly formed Republican Party was successful and that its candidate, Abraham Lincoln, came to occupy the White House. At the end of the election, the Democratic Party was bitterly divided, foreshadowing the sharp division that would soon lead to the Civil War.

5

WAR AND POLITICS

Shortly after Lincoln's inauguration, war broke out between the North and the South. Lincoln's party changed
its name from the Republican Party to the National Union
Party, and many Democrats joined it in a show of support
for the war effort. Others opposed the war and felt that the
South should be allowed to secede. These so-called "Peace
Democrats" were labeled "Copperheads" by their opponents, who accused them of behaving like snakes.

Lincoln was grateful for the support of the Democrats,
and when he sought reelection in 1864, he chose as his
vice president a former Democrat, Andrew Johnson of Tennessee. The Democrats chose a Union general, George
McClellan, as their nominee. McClellan's platform argued
for a negotiated settlement with the South—but the pres-
ence of many Democrats in Lincoln's National Union
Party helped to ensure Lincoln's reelection.

THE COPPERHEAD PARTY.——IN FAVOR OF *A VIGOROUS PROSECUTION OF PEACE!*

When war broke out between the North and the South, some Democrats opposed the war; they were labeled "Copperheads" by their opponents. In the cartoon above, the woman, Columbia (a poetic name for America), holds a shield labeled "Union," in order to defend herself from the caricatured Copperheads.

Johnson became president when Lincoln was assassinated. His administration was tarnished by scandal, though, and when he sought election in his own right, he faced both Republican opponents and a fierce challenge from the Democrats. He failed to win his party's nomination. Instead, it went to General Ulysses S. Grant. The Civil War had ended, and Democrats used racial prejudice as a way to frighten voters. They charged that Republican policies for rebuilding the South were intended to elevate former slaves above whites. Ultimately, the Democrats lost the election once again.

The Democrats failed to win the White House for 24 years. It was clear that the party needed new leadership and a new sense of direction. Not until 1884, with the nomination of Grover Cleveland, the former mayor of Buffalo and governor of New York, did the Democratic Party began to recover.

The party began an intensive campaign to restructure and reorganize. Workers were recruited not only at the national level, but also at the state, county, and local levels. Cities were the focus of much of this recruiting, and newly arrived Irish and Central European working-class immigrants were specifically targeted. Party workers would provide these immigrants with much-needed services (help them find jobs, arrange healthcare, and so on) in exchange for their votes.

Cleveland benefited from these efforts. He had worked hard to fight corruption, reform government, and reduce taxes. He and his Republican challenger, James Blaine, fought a bitter campaign, with scandals and gossip published to attack both sides. It was a close election, but Cleveland's New York electoral votes helped put him over the top.

Cleveland's two terms in office (one that began in 1884 and one 8 years later) would be the only times a Democrat served as president in a period of 52 years. From 1860 to 1912, the Republicans would, with only those two exceptions, hold on to the White House.

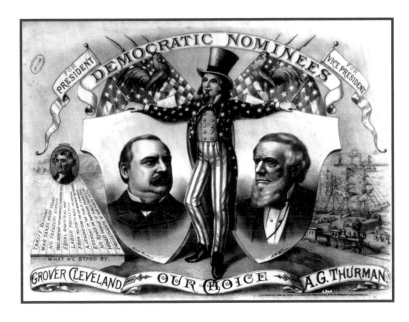

The Democrats failed to elect a president for 24 years after the Civil War, until Grover Cleveland was nominated in 1884. Above is a campaign illustration showing Cleveland and his running mate, A.G. Thurman.

Cleveland was nominated for a second term, but he failed to win the election against the Republican candidate, Benjamin Harrison. Cleveland won the popular vote, but not the electoral vote. The issue that had proved decisive involved tariffs (taxes) on imported goods. Cleveland challenged Harrison again in 1892, and, this time, he was up against a president weakened by poor financial management of the White House. Cleveland was elected, becoming the only president to serve two nonconsecutive terms.

Cleveland may have regretted his decision to return to the White House. Within two months of beginning his second term, the stock market collapsed. Banks and railroads began to fail, and thousands of businesses were forced to declare bankruptcy.

Cleveland stubbornly clung to his economic policies, even as Americans lost their jobs and pleaded for relief. The Cleveland administration's failures sparked further division in the Democratic Party. Once split into Northern and Southern wings, now disagreements separated residents of the Northeast from people living in the South and the West. Democrats who represented farm regions and those from industrial areas disagreed on policy, including whether the American monetary system should be based on a gold or a silver standard. Depression, strikes, and divisions in the party made it clear that a Democrat would not occupy the White House after Cleveland.

CROSS OF GOLD

In the presidential elections of 1896, 1900, and 1908, the Democratic nominee was William Jennings Bryan, a congressman from Nebraska. Bryan strongly supported an American money system based on silver rather than gold—a popular position in the West, where silver was mined.

In 1896, the debate over silver standard versus gold standard occupied the Democratic Party convention. Bryan delivered one of the most famous speeches in political history, arguing that the Democratic Party must stand on the side of rural Americans, of the "struggling masses." His speech ended with the dramatic words, "You shall not press down upon the brow of labor this crown of thorns; you shall not crucify mankind upon a cross of gold."

The speech made Bryan famous, and it brought him the nomination that year and in 1900 and 1908. Bryan would fail to win the presidency, losing to William McKinley in 1896 and 1900 and to William Taft in 1908. Still, Bryan's candidacy changed the image of the Democratic Party, shaping it once again into the party of the people.

Sixteen years passed without a Democrat in the White House, and that trend might have continued had it not been for division within the Republican Party. Republican president William Taft sought reelection in 1912, but his former friend and supporter, and former president, Theodore Roosevelt, decided to challenge Taft for the nomination. When he failed to win the Republican nomination, Roosevelt left the party and formed his own, the Progressive, or "Bull Moose," Party. This split in the Republicans was a boost to the Democratic Party and its candidate, Woodrow Wilson.

Wilson had only limited experience in politics and none at all at the national level. He had served as the president of Princeton University and had only recently won his first political election to become the governor of New Jersey. Wilson's campaign focused on what he called a plan for "New Freedom," which involved breaking up excessive power in the hands of big businesses in order to ensure protection for small businesses and farms to compete in the marketplace. Wilson campaigned feverishly, traveling by train from one small town to another and often making several stops and speeches a day. His pitch for the

Democratic Party as a progressive party and the split between the Republicans brought enough votes for Wilson
to become president.

As president, Wilson also took on the leadership of
the Democratic Party. He was determined to focus on his
"New Freedom" agenda, and, when World War I broke
out in Europe, he first stated that the United States would
remain neutral in the conflict. Wilson helped champion
several progressive laws, including those to ban child labor. His successes and the fact that America was not at
war helped win him reelection in 1920. Soon, however,
the sinking of three American merchant ships by German
forces made it impossible for Wilson to keep his promise of neutrality. He continued to work for peace while
preparing the country's military. When the war finally
ended, Wilson insisted on attending the peace conference
held in Paris, making him the first American president to
go abroad on a diplomatic mission. There, he signed the
Treaty of Versailles, the peace settlement following the ar-
mistice that ended World War I.

This treaty also founded an international organization called the League of Nations. This was Wilson's
brainchild, a forum that he felt would serve to preserve
the peace for future generations. But the U.S. Senate did
not ratify the treaty and the United States never joined
the League, leaving Wilson embarrassed and defeated.

Wilson kept his promise to support the right for women
to vote, and the constitutional amendment finally was
ratified in August 1920, in time for women to vote in the

The 1912 split in the Republican Party was a boon for the
Democratic Party, which had not elected a president for
16 years. Woodrow Wilson, pictured above, promoted the
Democratic Party as a progressive one.

presidential election. Still, the party failed to hold onto the presidency: Warren G. Harding easily defeated the Democratic nominee, Governor James Cox of Ohio, and his running mate, Assistant Secretary of the Navy Franklin Roosevelt.

Franklin Roosevelt began to work behind the scenes to help ensure reform of the Democratic Party. His belief was that the party was simply reacting to events in the Republican administration, hoping that the Republicans would make mistakes. Instead, he urged, the party needed to become more proactive, creating policies and shaping an agenda rather than responding to Republican policies.

In 1928, Roosevelt was elected governor of New York, launching him on the path that would lead to the White House. That path was made easier by the disastrous policies of Herbert Hoover, who was elected president in 1928, just before the nation's economy collapsed into the Great Depression. As Americans lost their jobs and their homes, Hoover continued to insist that relief should come at the local, not the national, level.

In New York, Governor Roosevelt created numerous programs to respond to the Depression, providing relief for the unemployed and focusing on plans for public works projects. Roosevelt's successful programs in New York won him the Democratic nomination in 1932.

Despite being in a wheelchair, Roosevelt campaigned vigorously and energetically, reassuring voters that the country needed to be rebuilt from the bottom up and that he would stand as the candidate for the "forgotten man."

At the Democratic convention, Roosevelt broke with the tradition of having candidates nominated in their absence. Instead, he took a small plane from Albany to Chicago (another noteworthy deed in those early days of flying, portraying him as a man of action) and arrived at the convention to accept the Democratic nomination in person.

Facing a country in economic crisis, President Hoover warned that Roosevelt's plans were not specific and lacked substance. The nation was desperate for change, however, and, on March 4, 1933, Franklin Delano Roosevelt became the thirty-second president of the United States.

Roosevelt's presidency would mark a dramatic turning point in the country's leadership and in the fortunes of the Democratic Party. Through dynamic leadership and creative policymaking, Roosevelt would win election to four terms as president and ensure that the White House remained in Democratic hands for 20 years.

6

A New Deal

During his inaugural speech, Franklin Roosevelt told the nation, "the only thing we have to fear is fear itself." His smiling face and take-charge manner demonstrated that he had confidence in his ability to help America rebuild after the crippling Depression.

Roosevelt's decisiveness was evident from the moment he assumed the presidency. Immediately after his inaugural parade, he had his cabinet sworn in all at the same time. He declared a four-day bank holiday, closing the banks and calling a special session of Congress to create emergency banking legislation. A few days later, he spoke to the nation on the radio, using a format he would make famous: the "fireside chat." He explained to everyone what he had done during the bank holiday and what he planned to do in the near future, asking Americans to return their savings to the banks when they reopened.

President Franklin D. Roosevelt talks to the nation in one of his famous fireside chats. Roosevelt introduced his radio talks to explain administration policies and to appeal to the people for support during the difficult 1930s.

During Roosevelt's first 100 days in office, he sent to Congress a series of emergency bills intended to address the country's economic crisis. Some of the bills focused on jobless relief to the states, others on cutbacks for government spending. There were bills to create the Civilian Conservation Corps and the Tennessee Valley Authority and others to protect home mortgages and reform railroads. Roosevelt spoke to the American public using his radio fireside chats to explain what he was doing, creating an atmosphere of confidence at a time when many were still out of work and worried about the future.

Roosevelt's successes gave the Democratic Party an opportunity to follow his model. Roosevelt's programs, called the "New Deal," also gave his party a new chance to identify itself as a party of optimism and change. He sponsored programs for better working conditions and supported union organizing, which resulted in strong union and worker support for the Democratic Party when Roosevelt sought reelection in 1936. It was in this campaign that political polling first became an important part of the election process. The Democratic Party surveyed voters not only on their choice for president but also on their views of Roosevelt's programs and policies. They could then use that information to target voters on the issues that mattered to them and to design better radio ads.

With this election, more voters identified themselves as supporters of the Democratic Party than ever before. For the first time, the Democratic Party was able to claim solid support from African Americans (a significant change— previously, they had supported the Republican Party of Abraham Lincoln) and from farmers; both groups felt that they had benefited from legislation championed by Roosevelt. The Democrats also profited from the support of unions, the unemployed (who believed that Roosevelt's policies would help them soon), and immigrants.

Roosevelt won reelection, but his plan to reorganize the Supreme Court prompted conservatives within his own party to protest. By 1940, Hitler's army was on the march, and Europe was enmeshed in war. Roosevelt decided that the global events made it critical for the United States to have an experienced leader, despite the fact that no American president had served more than two terms. Roosevelt made it clear to leading Democrats that he would accept the party's nomination for a third term if it was offered to him. It was.

Roosevelt told the nation that he needed to remain at the White House rather than spend time in political debates. His Republican opponent, Wendell Wilkie, took advantage of Roosevelt's absence on the campaign trail by crisscrossing the country, outlining his vision for the future. Wilkie had once been a Democrat himself—in fact, he had voted for Roosevelt in 1932. Wilkie's campaign suggested that Roosevelt was trying to create a monarchy in America, with Roosevelt as its king.

Roosevelt reassured the American public that "your boys are not going to be sent into foreign wars," a promise he claimed to have kept after the United States entered World War II. The Japanese attack on Pearl Harbor was an attack on U.S. soil, he reasoned, meaning that the war could not be described as "foreign."

Roosevelt won a decisive victory over Wilkie. Less than a year after he began his third term, the United States entered World War II. Gradually, the war began to turn in the favor of the United States and its allies, and by 1944 Roosevelt's image as a confident commander in chief made it possible for him to consider a fourth term as president.

After the 1940 campaign, Wilkie and Roosevelt mended their relationship and discussed an interesting possibility. Both the Republican and Democratic parties had conservatives who had more in common with each other than with more liberal members. Both men were frustrated by the conservative members of their respective parties—particularly by their unwillingness to consider change. The men discussed a dramatic proposal: to completely remake the Democratic and Republican parties into two new political parties, one conservative and one liberal. The two men apparently hoped that their new party system might be put into place by 1948. By 1948, however, both Wilkie and Roosevelt were dead. In the following decades, the parties would eventually shift, with the Republican Party becoming the party of conservatives and the Democratic Party attracting liberals.

HARRY TRUMAN

When running for his fourth term as president in 1944, Roosevelt decided to change his vice president. Roosevelt chose Senator Harry S. Truman of Missouri as his running mate. With a modest amount of campaigning, Roosevelt defeated his Republican opponent, Thomas Dewey.

Within six months of taking office for the fourth time, Roosevelt was dead, having suffered a cerebral hemorrhage. Truman became president. Truman faced the challenge of filling the shoes of the man who had occupied the Oval Office longer than any other and who had dramatically reshaped the Democratic Party and its policies. The party for which Truman was now the symbol was focused on new and challenging issues, many of which would occupy it for most of the century—civil rights, foreign policy, and the expanding role of the federal government. It was becoming a party concentrated in Northern cities and dependent on the support of immigrants and labor, as well as that of African-American voters.

Truman made the difficult decision to use the atomic bomb on Japan to bring an end to World War II. In the years immediately after the war, conflict with the Soviet Union led to concern about the possible spread of Communism, and the American economy faltered. Truman faced opposition within his party, and Republicans saw real opportunity to recapture the White House after 16 years. They again chose Thomas Dewey of New York as their presidential candidate.

The election of 1948 was the first time presidential party conventions were televised. The audiences were generally small, and events were not planned to coincide with television coverage in the way that speeches and events today are scheduled to play during prime-time hours. Certain members of the Democratic Party made an appeal to General Dwight Eisenhower, the leader of the Allied troops in Europe, to challenge Truman for the nomination, but Eisenhower refused.

This cleared the way for Truman to be nominated. Civil rights became a major issue for the party platform. At the convention, the mayor of Minneapolis, Hubert Humphrey, who was at the time in a race for the Senate to represent Minnesota, made a speech that urged Democrats to "get out of the shadow of states' rights and walk forthrightly into the bright sunshine of human rights."

When President Roosevelt died in 1944, Harry S. Truman, his vice president, took over. Truman inherited leadership of a radically reshaped Democratic Party. Though some in his own party opposed him, he was reelected to the presidency in 1948.

DIXIECRATS

There were many, particularly Southern, delegates within the Democratic Party who disagreed with this commitment to civil rights and with Truman's executive order to desegregate the armed forces. Some left the party, gathered in Birmingham, Alabama, and nominated their own candidate for president, Governor J. Strom Thurmond of South Carolina, on the "States' Rights Democratic Party" ticket. These "States' Rights Democrats" (also known as

Dixiecrats) supported a platform based on racial segregation. The Dixiecrats were able to have their ticket declared the official Democratic ticket in Alabama, Louisiana, Mississippi, and South Carolina, and ultimately won in these four states.

Early polls predicted that Dewey would be the winner, but Truman pulled off an upset and managed to retain the presidency for the Democrats. The Dixiecrats disappeared as a separate political party, but their impact was clear. Disillusioned with the Democratic Party and its position on civil rights, many Dixiecrats would eventually join the Republican Party, including the man who ran for the presidency on the States' Rights Democratic Party ticket, Strom Thurmond.

A FAIR DEAL

In his inaugural speech, Truman described the role of his administration: to ensure that Americans were given a "fair deal." A twist on Roosevelt's "New Deal," the "Fair Deal" promised new action in civil rights, government aid to public education, and national health insurance. Truman's Fair Deal also requested higher social security payments and an increase in the minimum wage.

Truman had hoped to focus on domestic policy in this new term, but events in the world soon made that impossible. Tensions with the Soviet Union raised fears of Communist influence throughout the world. When North Korea invaded South Korea, the president ordered U.S. troops into the conflict as part of a United Nations force.

Truman himself decided that nearly eight years in office was enough. In a campaign in which primaries were becoming increasingly important (1952), Truman urged support for the Democratic candidate he liked best—Governor Adlai Stevenson of Illinois. Stevenson was witty and articulate, but he was little match for his popular opponent, Republican Dwight D. Eisenhower, the general whom Democrats had hoped to draft as their nominee only a few years earlier. This was the first presidential campaign in which paid television advertising played an important role; the ads for Eisenhower proclaimed "I like Ike," whereas Stevenson seemed too intellectual to many voters. Republicans effectively labeled Democrats the party of "Korea, Communism, and Corruption," bringing an end to 20 years of Democratic rule.

WINDS OF CHANGE

The next eight years represented a time of transition and change within the Democratic Party. Eisenhower suffered a heart attack near the end of his first term. His vice president, Richard Nixon, was unpopular, and the Democrats hoped that the possibility of his becoming president if Eisenhower's health failed might win voters who wanted to prevent that to their side. Eisenhower recovered, however, and Adlai Stevenson (once again the Democratic candidate) failed to take a significant number of votes from the popular president in 1956.

By 1960, a new candidate had emerged to challenge the Republican candidate, Vice President Nixon, for the presidency. John F. Kennedy, a senator from Massachusetts, had given a stirring speech at the 1956 Democratic convention and was the kind of handsome and charismatic candidate that the party needed. Kennedy's candidacy faced some challenges: He was young (if elected, he would be only 43 years old at his inauguration) and he was Catholic. No Catholic had ever been elected president, and the religious bias of that time forced Kennedy to make it clear that he would make policy based on what was best for the United States, not what was best for the Catholic Church.

As his running mate, Kennedy chose a man who had opposed him for the Democratic nomination: Speaker of the House Lyndon B. Johnson of Texas. Kennedy had offered Johnson the nomination as a courtesy and was somewhat shocked when he accepted.

The contrast between the Republican and Democratic parties was dramatically illustrated by their respective candidates in 1960. Richard Nixon, the vice president, had built his conservative reputation on his deep suspicion of Communists and his willingness to serve as Eisenhower's attack dog during their campaigns. In a campaign speech, Nixon had foolishly promised to visit all 50 states, a pledge that would force him into an exhausting series of campaign appearances while Kennedy was free to focus on the states that were most critical to his victory.

During the campaign, Kennedy learned that civil rights leader Martin Luther King Jr. had been arrested in Georgia and sentenced to four months of hard labor. He called King's wife to ask what he could do to help. The call and the pressure Kennedy then put on Georgia authorities to

Richard Nixon *(left)* and John F. Kennedy are shown in a photograph from one of the 1960 presidential campaign debates. The televised debates strongly influenced the election. Kennedy's youthful, handsome appearance was particularly appealing to voters.

release King prompted strong support for Kennedy among African Americans.

A series of televised debates played a critical role in the 1960 election. Kennedy was tanned and rested and appeared relaxed and confident on camera. Nixon, on the other hand, seemed uncomfortable, and his sweat was visible to the television audience. The election was close, but in the end Kennedy won, giving the Democrats the go-ahead to set out toward what Kennedy had described as the "New Frontier."

A NEW ERA

Kennedy began his presidency with confidence and enthusiasm, and the country quickly rallied behind the president and his glamorous young wife. The Kennedys' young children roamed through the White House. Kennedy brought with him a staff of well-educated, committed young men and women dedicated to public service.

Kennedy urged support for the U.S. space program and, less successfully, for civil rights. He also launched the Peace Corps. When the Soviets placed missiles in nearby Cuba, Kennedy made it clear that the situation would not be accepted. The Soviets were finally forced to back down and remove the missiles. It was also during the Kennedy administration that the U.S. role in Vietnam began to widen, with what would prove to be disastrous consequences for future presidents. American troops were sent as "advisers" to the government in South Vietnam, to assist in its efforts to resist Communist attacks from North Vietnam. Kennedy had indicated his interest in eventually pulling the troops out, planning to do it in his second term.

In November 1963, Kennedy traveled to Texas, in part to help settle a disagreement between two key members of the Democratic Party there, Governor John Connally and U.S. Senator Ralph Yarborough. By publicly appearing around the state with both politicians, Kennedy hoped to heal their disagreement (at least publicly) and also to ensure Texas votes for his planned bid for reelection in 1964. On November 22, while traveling in a motorcade through Dallas, Kennedy was shot. He died shortly afterward.

His vice president, Lyndon Johnson, faced the difficult task of filling the shoes of the popular leader who had brought glamour to the White House and inspiration to many young voters. Johnson made it clear from the beginning that he intended to continue Kennedy's legacy. From this promise, the so-called "Great Society" was born.

7

CHANGING SOCIETY

Johnson was committed to continuing the plans set out by Kennedy during his presidency. He quickly shepherded a tax cut and a civil rights bill to bar discrimination in public accommodations. He outlined his plans for a "Great Society" in which opportunity would be shared by all Americans. His policies as part of this "Great Society" included farm aid, food stamps, systems of transit for cities, anticrime bills, housing acts, and more. Johnson also announced the launch of a "War on Poverty." He championed the Job Corps for school dropouts and Head Start for preschool children.

The war on Vietnam took some of Johnson's focus away from his domestic programs, however. The situation in South Korea was increasingly unstable, and rather than

After Democratic president John F. Kennedy was assassinated, his vice president, Lyndon B. Johnson *(above)*, assumed the presidency. He continued Kennedy's programs and was reelected in 1964.

following Kennedy's plan for a troop withdrawal, Johnson increased the number of attacks against North Vietnam.

Johnson ran as the Democratic nominee for the presidency in 1964. His opponent was Senator Barry Goldwater, known for his outspoken anti-Communist views and his adversarial position toward China and Russia. Playing on fears that Goldwater might launch a nuclear war with one of the two Communist nations, Johnson spoke of working toward easing tensions with the Soviet Union. Television commercials for the Democratic candidate emphasized him as the candidate working for peace. He won a commanding victory; the Republicans won only Goldwater's home state of Arizona and five Southern states.

With such a firm victory and Democratic control of both the House and Senate, Johnson was able to push through even more legislation to help shape the "Great Society," including Medicare, aid to secondary and higher education, low-income housing, and a new Voting Rights Act. New government initiatives included the Department of Housing and Urban Development and the Department of Transportation. Once, the federal budget had been focused largely on military expenses, but now welfare-related expenses began to consume more of the federal revenue.

America was at a crossroads, though, and the great society Johnson dreamed of would soon confront the reality of an increasingly militant and violent population. Black Muslims began to openly discuss black separatism and self-defense. When their spokesman, Malcolm X, began to speak of unity among the races instead, he was murdered. A march to register voters in Alabama led by Martin Luther King Jr. was attacked by state troopers in Selma. Race riots happened in large and small cities, and the war in Vietnam continued to kill Americans and spark protests, many of them on college campuses.

It was increasingly difficult for President Johnson to travel anywhere without tight security and prescreened audiences for his speeches. Protests erupted wherever he appeared, and antiwar marchers picketed outside the White House.

In 1968, Senator Eugene McCarthy of Minnesota announced his intention to challenge the president for the Democratic nomination. McCarthy's antiwar position appealed to young voters, who rallied behind his cause and began to work for his campaign. In the first primary, in New Hampshire, McCarthy won nearly as many votes as the president. After McCarthy's successful challenge, Senator Robert Kennedy of Massachusetts, brother of the former president, also decided to seek the Democratic nomination.

On March 31, 1968, Johnson went on television to deliver a speech about the Vietnam War. He spoke for nearly 45 minutes about the recent bombing of North Vietnam, his decision to send 13,500 more American troops over the next five months, and the funds that would be spent to equip South Vietnamese troops. Then, without advance warning, Johnson concluded his speech with the shocking announcement that he would not seek another term as president.

TURMOIL IN THE PARTY

Johnson's surprising announcement threw the party into chaos. Four days later, Martin Luther King Jr. was assassinated. His murder was followed by riots in more than 100 cities.

Johnson's vice president, Hubert Humphrey, now decided to seek the Democratic nomination. The three candidates—McCarthy, Kennedy, and Humphrey—struggled to position themselves on the issues. Humphrey faced the most difficult challenge: He inherited the problems of the Johnson administration and was unable to distance himself from Johnson's policies without appearing disloyal. Robert Kennedy won the critical California primary, but as he made his way to the press conference after his victory, he was shot and killed. Antiwar protests intensified.

The Democratic Party convention, held in Chicago in 1968, would go down in history as one of the most violent and chaotic political conventions ever held. Chicago's mayor, Richard Daley, had ordered the convention center surrounded by barbed wire and a chain-link fence. City police and members of the Illinois National Guard scrutinized the delegates as they entered the convention. This did not stop the protestors from gathering outside and clashing with police, who responded by clubbing protestors with nightsticks and throwing them into police vans.

Inside, the atmosphere was every bit as fierce. Supporters of McCarthy chanted "stop the war" and insisted that the Democratic platform contain a clause that called for an immediate end to the bombing in North Vietnam and a negotiated withdrawal of all American troops. Humphrey's supporters argued for a bombing halt only if troops in the field were not endangered and for withdrawal after the war had ended. The points were debated for three hours before Humphrey's platform was adopted.

The convention proved to be a boon to the Republicans and their candidate, former vice president Richard Nixon. Images of the violence outside the Democratic convention, the anger and screaming inside, the race riots, and the war protests, helped Nixon's campaign as a "law and order" candidate, a candidate who would return America to the peace of the Eisenhower years.

As a last-minute candidate, Humphrey had not carved out a strategy for combating the Republicans or distinguishing himself from Johnson. Although Nixon did not give many specifics about how he would deal with Vietnam, Humphrey was constantly questioned about the war and asked how his policies would differ from Johnson's.

A third candidate also ran for the presidency in 1968. Governor George Wallace of Alabama ran on the American Reform Party ticket. His television commercials focused on the need to end school busing and increase public safety. The subtext of his speeches was a racial prejudice that was clear to his listeners.

In the end, the violence in the streets, the protests and riots, and the disastrous images of the Vietnam War prompted a Democratic defeat. Richard Nixon won the White House and inherited many of the problems that had plagued his Democratic predecessor.

The 1968 Democratic convention became notorious for the demonstrations, both inside and out, that disrupted business. Above, police lead a demonstrator away from Grant Park in Chicago, where the convention was held.

1970s

Richard Nixon won the election by portraying himself as a candidate for law and order. He also implied that he had a "secret plan" to end the Vietnam War. By 1970, however, he had in fact expanded the war, sending American troops into the neighboring country of Cambodia, which immediately sparked a fierce round of antiwar protests.

The country was sharply divided into young and old, liberal and conservative, antiwar and anticommunist. By 1971, George McGovern, a senator from South Dakota, had announced his decision to seek the Democratic Party nomination. He was one of many Democrats who sought the nomination, including Hubert Humphrey and the first female African-American candidate for president, Congresswoman Shirley Chisholm of New York.

Shortly before the New York primary, a break-in was reported at the Democratic National Committee headquarters in the Watergate building complex in Washington, D.C. Police caught five men attempting to burglarize the office of the Democratic Party chairman, and it was soon learned that the five were all connected to the Republican Committee to Reelect the President. Nixon and his aides denied any connection or involvement. Their statements were proved false—after the election.

McGovern won the Democratic nomination, thanks in large part to his antiwar platform, which called for complete U.S. withdrawal from Vietnam and reduction in military spending. McGovern's choice as his running mate was Senator Thomas Eagleton of Missouri, who later revealed that he had been hospitalized and received shock therapy for depression. McGovern at first announced support for Eagleton but later decided to replace him with former ambassador Sargent Shriver. This decision made the Democratic Party look indecisive, and Nixon effectively portrayed the Democrats as a party of "long-haired" liberals who would weaken America militarily and in the eyes of the world. Nixon also stressed that peace was "at hand."

Nixon won every state except Massachusetts. He had appealed not only to Republicans but also to traditionally Democratic groups like laborers, Catholics, Jews, and African Americans.

The victory proved short-lived. Vice President Spiro Agnew was forced to resign when it was learned that he had accepted payoffs from Maryland contractors and evaded income tax payments. House Minority Leader Gerald Ford was named the new vice president.

In February 1974, the House Judiciary Committee began an investigation into Nixon's involvement with Watergate. Evidence on the secretly-recorded tapes made it clear that the president had been involved in the break-in and in the cover-up that followed. Nixon learned he was likely to face impeachment, and he decided to resign.

Ford took office promising change and a clean slate. His support quickly disappeared when, one month after becoming president, he issued a complete pardon for Nixon. He made the decision to spare the country the turmoil of seeing its former president on trial, but it doomed Ford's chances to seek the presidency in 1976.

The Watergate break-in and the televised hearings that followed shook most Americans' confidence in their government. The Vietnam War came to a disastrous close with American troops withdrawing in defeat.

The issues that dominated the 1976 presidential race were integrity and character. A number of candidates vied for the Democratic nomination, and Governor Jimmy Carter of Georgia succeeded. His campaign focused on his status as a Washington outsider, a man of honor and character, a graduate of the naval academy, and a hard-working farmer—the first farmer to seek the presidency since Jefferson, according to some campaign ads. Carter positioned himself as a "centrist," with policies and ideas that straddled the line between liberal and conservative. He promised in his campaign never to lie to the American people.

The election was close, but the Democrats won, taking back the White House after eight years of Republican domination.

FOUR TROUBLED YEARS

Carter took office with the promise of a fresh start and a government that could be trusted; however, his four years in office were marked by poor decisions and mismanagement. Carter's status as an outsider made it difficult for him to form the kind of alliances that help bills pass through Congress and to ensure that an agenda can be carried out.

Carter had no foreign policy experience, making it even more difficult for him to assess and respond to events around the world. Efforts to negotiate an arms-control treaty with the Soviet Union failed. He did successfully negotiate a Middle East peace treaty between Israel and Egypt, but the U.S. economy faltered and the country was beset by an energy crisis, with Americans forced to wait in long lines at gas stations simply to put gasoline in their cars. Rationing was introduced: A person could only purchase gasoline on certain days, based on the odd or even numbers in his or her license plate, and Americans were told to turn down their thermostats and bundle up to save heating oil.

In 1976, Democrat Jimmy Carter took the White House with promises of a fresh start and a government that could be trusted. Ultimately, however, his presidency was doomed by numerous crises, including an energy shortage and Americans held as hostages in Iran.

A revolution in Iran would prove to be the most decisive blow to Carter's presidency. When the ruler of Iran, the shah, was forced out of the country after a revolution that ushered in a fundamentalist Islamic regime, he asked to be allowed into the United States to seek medical treatment. Carter's decision to admit the shah triggered the seizure of the American embassy in Iran's capital, Tehran, and the capture of 66 Americans as hostages. A failed attempt to rescue the hostages ended in disaster, conveying to Americans an image of their country as incompetent and helpless, even to protect its own citizens.

Carter received the nomination of the Democratic Party when he sought reelection. He was challenged by a former actor and governor of California, Ronald Reagan, whose Republican campaign highlighted Carter's mistakes and promised a return to a strong America. Reagan campaigned on a pledge to stand tough against the Soviet Union and against anyone who would challenge America. He promised to bring an end to the country's economic woes and to restore Americans' pride in their country. Republican congressman John Anderson of Illinois also entered the race on the National Unity Party ticket.

As the hostage crisis dragged on for month after month, with efforts at negotiating their release proving futile, Carter's popularity began to drop in the polls. The Republican campaign effectively targeted the Democratic president by posing the question, "Are you better off than you were four years ago?" For most Americans, the answer was "no."

Jimmy Carter became the first Democratic incumbent to lose a bid for reelection since Grover Cleveland in 1888. The Iranians released the hostages shortly after Ronald Reagan's inauguration, a final blow to the Democratic president.

The 1980 election marked a fundamental shift in American politics. Ronald Reagan and the Republicans had accurately read the sentiment of many Americans: They wanted a more conservative government. With what came to be known as the "Reagan Revolution," a new era began, one in which many of the policies launched by Democratic presidents like Roosevelt and Johnson would gradually be abandoned.

8

THE MODERN DEMOCRATIC PARTY

From 1980 to 1992, Democrats failed to capture the White House. Reagan's policies—cutting taxes and reducing many federal programs that helped the poor and unemployed while increasing military spending—served to jump-start the economy.

For eight years, Reagan controlled the White House. His vice president, George H.W. Bush, was elected to the presidency in 1988. In 1984, Carter's vice president, Walter Mondale, ran as the Democratic challenger to the incumbent Reagan. Mondale failed to capture voters' support, even with his choice of running mate, Geraldine

In 1984, the Democrats nominated Walter Mondale. His running mate, Geraldine Ferraro, was the first female vice-presidential candidate for a major party. Above, Ferraro *(left)* and Mondale *(right)* wave to the crowd at a campaign event.

Ferraro—the first female vice-presidential candidate for a major party. Mondale won only a single state, his home state of Minnesota, in the most lopsided election since 1936. In 1988, Massachusetts governor Michael Dukakis also failed in his effort to recapture the White House for the Democrats. His plans for increased government spending on health care, education, child care, and housing allowed Vice President Bush to depict Dukakis as a typical "tax-and-spend" Democrat. Defining himself as the heir to the Reagan tradition, Bush won a decisive victory.

The Democrats had failed in three consecutive elections. Their traditional programs, based on support for the disadvantaged and the needy, had proved unsuccessful. It was clear that the Democratic Party needed to redefine itself, and its candidates, if it was ever to recapture the White House.

In 1991, President George H.W. Bush oversaw a successful effort to force Iraqi leader Saddam Hussein out of nearby Kuwait in a military campaign known as Operation Desert Storm. After the victory, Bush's approval ratings soared to nearly 90 percent. He seemed unbeatable, and many wary Democratic candidates who had been considering a run for the White House decided to postpone their efforts until after the 1992 election. It seemed clear that Bush would easily win reelection.

In the midst of this, Governor Bill Clinton of Arkansas won the 1992 Democratic Party nomination. Clinton wisely chose to position himself as a centrist. As the campaign season began, the American economy began to falter and the Clinton campaign focused on this issue. Signs at the Clinton campaign headquarters reminded staffers, "It's the economy, stupid."

As his running mate, Clinton chose another young Southern Democrat—Al Gore of Tennessee. The two traveled around the country by bus, representing themselves as a "new generation of Democrats" who called for an "end to welfare as we know it," support for the death penalty, and a rejection of "tax-and-spend politics." Suddenly, the Democrats were beginning to sound a lot like the Republicans.

Texas billionaire Ross Perot also challenged President Bush on the economy, representing what he called the

Reform Party. Televised debates worked to Clinton's advantage, and Clinton successfully targeted both lower- and middle-income voters with his policies. Questions were raised about Clinton's marriage and his reluctance to serve in Vietnam, but Bush's candidacy was harmed by an appearance in a supermarket in which the president seemed out of touch.

In the end, Clinton won a slim majority of 43 percent of the votes. Even third-party candidate Perot performed strongly, winning 19 percent of the popular vote. Clinton had succeeded in reshaping the Democratic Party to appeal to new voters, recognizing the desire for change while positioning himself as a "New Democrat."

THE COMEBACK KID

Clinton's first few months in office were marked by a series of embarrassing stumbles. He failed to win support for his dramatic plan to reform health care and was forced to withdraw several early candidates for his cabinet when questions were raised about their backgrounds. His decision to fire longtime officials in the White House travel office and replace them with an Arkansas travel agency was also controversial.

Criticisms were made that Clinton, while claiming to be a "New Democrat," was secretly the same old liberal Democrat. Midterm elections brought a severe rebuke to the Clinton White House, as Republicans took control of both the House and the Senate.

Clinton wisely decided to shift back to the center, proposing what he called a "Middle Class Bill of Rights" that

Arkansas Governor Bill Clinton won the Democratic nomination for president in 1992. He won the election after positioning himself in the political center and focusing on the faltering American economy.

featured a middle-income tax cut. His policies focused not on an increased role for government (the traditional policy for Democratic presidents) but instead on individuals, on what was described as "opportunity with responsibility." He proposed a balanced budget plan—this budget plan would ultimately lead to a showdown with House of Representatives Speaker Newt Gingrich, which resulted in a temporary shutdown of the government. As the 1996 election drew closer, Clinton declared, "The era of big government is over."

With a healthy economy and the Republicans successfully depicted as "extreme," Clinton won reelection. The Democratic platform had reflected Clinton's "New Democrat" focus, with plans for welfare legislation, deficit reduction, tougher anticrime bills, middle-class tax cuts, and a balanced budget.

Clinton's second term began on a strong note. Many Democrats now defined themselves as "New Democrats" in the Clinton mold. The economy was healthy, and the United States was at peace.

There were ongoing questions about Clinton's personal and financial conduct, however, which ultimately led to an investigation. The investigation suggested that Clinton had had an inappropriate relationship with a White House intern, a charge that Clinton at first denied and then was forced to acknowledge. On December 19, 1998, the House voted to impeach Clinton on charges of perjury and obstruction of justice. The House vote fell along party lines, with Republicans leading the charge to impeach the president. The impeachment process then moved to the Senate for trial, where Clinton was acquitted of the charges.

For his remaining two years in office, Clinton focused on building his legacy—but the trial and the scandals uncovered by the investigation would haunt his presidency and set a bad precedent for Vice President Al Gore when he sought the presidency in 2000.

A BITTER FIGHT

The 2000 election focused almost exclusively on domestic issues—things like prescription drug plans for senior citizens, the economy, social security, and education. Al Gore was challenged by Republican governor George W. Bush of Texas, the son of former president George H.W. Bush. Learning from the successes of Clinton and the "New Democrats," both candidates positioned themselves at the center, avoiding the more extreme positions of members of their respective parties. George W. Bush campaigned as a "compassionate conservative," and Al Gore focused on his plans to strengthen education and protect the environment.

The election was the closest in American history, prompting a recount of votes in Florida that left the question of who would be the next president of the United States unanswered for 36 days. A controversial Supreme Court decision finally brought the recount to an end, and George W. Bush was declared the winner.

With the beginning of his presidency under a cloud, it seemed possible to many Democrats that Bush, like his father, would be a one-term president. Then the terrorist attacks on America on September 11, 2001, changed the political climate, at least temporarily. Bush was able to rally the nation against those who had attacked it and to inspire Democrats to join with Republicans in his decision to attack those responsible—the al Qaeda terrorist network, based in Afghanistan.

The president's decision to expand the war on terrorism into Iraq gradually eroded the bipartisan support he had enjoyed. The Bush administration presented evidence that suggested a possible link between al Qaeda and Iraqi leader Saddam Hussein and charged Hussein with attempting to stockpile biological, chemical, and nuclear weapons.

The evidence of this connection would later prove faulty, however. Although a U.S.-led coalition of troops was able to defeat the Iraqi army quickly and ultimately capture Hussein, the country erupted in violence. Questions about the U.S. involvement in Iraq became one of the central issues of the 2004 election, as Democratic senator John Kerry of Massachusetts challenged President Bush in his bid for reelection. For the first time in many years, the election focused on terrorism and foreign policy, with the economy and domestic issues playing a minor role.

In the 2004 election, the Democratic and Republican candidates returned, in a sense, to the positions that had defined their parties for many years. The Republican candidate, President Bush, focused on his role as

the experienced, steady commander in chief, a leader
equipped to handle a dangerous and uncertain world.
Democratic Party candidate Kerry stressed his connec-

STRONG AT HOME, RESPECTED IN THE WORLD

The 2004 Democratic National platform, titled "Strong at
Home, Respected in the World," reflected concerns about
America's safety after the September 11, 2001, attacks while
promising a "new direction." The platform included a nod to the
party's history:

> . . . Our vision has deep roots in our Declaration
> of Independence and Franklin Delano Roosevelt's
> Four Freedoms, and in the tough-minded tradition
> of engagement and leadership—a tradition forged by
> Wilson and Roosevelt in two world wars, then cham-
> pioned by Truman and Kennedy during the Cold
> War. We believe in an America that people around
> the world admire, because they know we cherish not
> just our freedom, but theirs. Not just our democracy,
> but their hope for it. Not just our peace and secu-
> rity, but the world's. We believe in an America that
> cherishes freedom, safeguards our people, forges al-
> liances, and commands respect. That is the America
> we are going to build. . . .

Source: The Democratic Party. Available online. URL: http://www
.democrats.org.

tion to the concerns of average Americans. Concerns about safety played a key role for many voters, though, and President Bush was able to win reelection.

THE DEMOCRATIC PARTY TODAY

In the more than 200 years of its existence, the Democratic Party has undergone dramatic changes. It began as the party of Thomas Jefferson, challenging the Federalists and focusing on greater power for the states and an economy based on farms and plantations. Under Andrew Jackson, it became a party of the ordinary American and then nearly crumbled under the divisive issue of slavery. The party struggled to shape its identity in the years after the Civil War, emerging after World War I as a party that favored a leading role for the United States in international politics.

With Franklin Roosevelt, the Democratic Party became a champion of a government that was responsive to the needs of the people, a trend that continued under Lyndon Johnson. Under Bill Clinton, the party moved back to the center, eliminating some of the social programs that had once brought the party to power and focusing instead on the idea of a smaller, more efficient government.

The Democratic Party had once been the party of white voters, a party with its strongest support in the South. Gradually, its strength shifted to cities in the Northeast and Midwest and to blue-collar, minority, and immigrant workers. In the 1950 and 1960s, more responsive civil rights policies increased the Democratic Party's appeal to African-American voters and, later, to women.

On its Web site, the Democratic Party states that its goal is to achieve "a secure nation that leads in the world, strong economic growth and new jobs, affordable health care for all Americans, and a better education for our children." The party outlines a "6-Point Plan" to carry out its mission: honest leadership and open government, real security, energy independence, economic prosperity and educational excellence, a health care system that works for everyone, and retirement security. These issues will likely form the Democratic Party's agenda as it prepares for future elections.

The Democratic Party began its history as "the party of the common man." The challenge for the oldest political party in American history is to continue to reflect the hopes and dreams of ordinary Americans while shaping an effective vision for the nation.

GLOSSARY

abolitionist   An activist who works to outlaw slavery.

aristocracy   A select or elite group within a society noted for its wealth and property.

ballot   A system used for voting for a candidate.

caucus   A meeting held to nominate candidates for a particular political office and to decide a political party's policies.

Communism   A political movement designed to use revolutionary methods to achieve a classless society in which all goods and property are owned by the society rather than by the individual.

Copperhead   A critical term used to describe Democrats who supported a negotiated settlement with the South at the time of the Civil War.

democracy   A political system in which the people direct the activities of their government, either directly or through representatives.

depression   A period of economic crisis in which prices fall, unemployment rises, and businesses may be forced to close.

Electoral College   A group of representatives from each of the states who meet and vote for a particular candidate.

electoral votes   Votes in the Electoral College; the number of electoral votes a state has is based on the number of senators and representatives it has.

liberal   A political philosophy that focuses on individual rights and favors greater government involvement in providing for the welfare of its citizens.

mid-term elections   In the United States, elections in which members of Congress, some state governors, and representatives to state legislatures are elected, but not the president; an election that takes place in the middle of a presidential term.

Monroe Doctrine   A foreign policy developed by President James Monroe that stated that the United States would support efforts by former Spanish and Portuguese colonies in Latin America to achieve independence and oppose any efforts by foreign powers to colonize lands in the Western Hemisphere.

party platform   The stated goals and policies of a political party.

popular vote   A system in which citizens directly cast their votes for a candidate; the candidate who receives the most votes from citizens wins the election.

progressive   Favoring change, improvement, or reform.

secede   To leave or withdraw from a group or organization; this term is often used to describe the decision of Southern states to leave the Union shortly before the Civil War.

tariff   A tax placed mainly on imported goods; designed to protect a country's businesses, industries, or manufacturers from foreign competition.

ticket   In politics, two or more candidates nominated by a party who run together in an election.

BIBLIOGRAPHY

Brown, Stuart G. *The First Republicans: Political Philosophy and Public Policy in the Party of Jefferson and Madison.* Syracuse, N.Y.: Syracuse University Press, 1954.

Cunningham, Noble E., Jr. *The Jeffersonian Republicans: The Formation of Party Organization, 1789–1801.* Chapel Hill, N.C.: The University of North Carolina Press, 1957.

———. *The Jeffersonian Republicans in Power: Party Operations, 1801–1809.* Chapel Hill, N.C.: The University of North Carolina Press, 1963.

Goldman, Ralph M. *The Democratic Party in American Politics.* New York: The Macmillan Company, 1966.

Judis, John B. *The Emerging Democratic Majority.* New York: Scribner, 2002.

Kent, Frank R. *The Democratic Party: A History.* New York: The Century Co., 1928.

Remini, Robert V. *Martin Van Buren and the Making of the Democratic Party.* New York: Columbia University Press, 1959.

Rutland, Robert Allen. *The Democrats: From Jefferson to Clinton.* Columbia, Mo.: The University of Missouri Press, 1995.

Sarasohn, David. *The Party of Reform: Democrats in the Progressive Era.* Jackson, Miss.: University Press of Mississippi, 1989.

Silbey, Joel H. *A Respectable Minority: The Democratic Party in the Civil War Era 1860–1868.* New York: Norton, 1977.

Witcover, Jules. *Party of the People: A History of the Democrats.* New York: Random House, 2003.

Web Sites

American President: An Online Reference Resource, University of Virginia: Miller Center of Public Affairs
http://www.americanpresident.org

The Democratic Party
http://www.democrats.org

"Election of 1800," C-SPAN.org
http://www.c-span.org/classroom/govt/1800.asp

The Living Room Candidate
http://livingroomcandidate.movingimage.us

Profiles of U.S. Presidents
http://www.presidentprofiles.com

"Thomas Jefferson First Inaugural Address," The Avalon Project at Yale Law School
http://www.yale.edu/lawweb/avalon/presiden/inaug/jefinau1.htm

FURTHER READING

Anderson, Catherine Corley. *John F. Kennedy*. Minneapolis, Minn.: Lerner Publications, 2004.

Bober, Natalie S. *Thomas Jefferson: Man on a Mountain*. New York: Aladdin, 1997.

Colbert, Nancy A. *Great Society: The Story of Lyndon Baines Johnson*. Greensboro, N.C.: Morgan Reynolds, 2002.

Collier, Christopher. *Progressivism, The Great Depression, and the New Deal, 1901–1941*. New York: Benchmark Books, 2000.

Freedman, Russell. *Franklin Delano Roosevelt*. New York: Clarion Books, 1990.

Kronenwetter, Michael. *Political Parties of the United States*. Berkeley Heights, N.J.: Enslow Publishers, 1996.

Saffell, David C. (ed.). *The Encyclopedia of U.S. Presidential Elections*. New York: Franklin Watts, 2004.

Web Sites

The American Presidency
http://ap.grolier.com

Annenberg Political Fact Check
http://www.factcheck.org

The Democratic Party
http://www.democrats.org

The Living Room Candidate
http://livingroomcandidate.movingimage.us

Monticello: The Home of Thomas Jefferson
http://www.monticello.org

The White House: The Presidents of the United States
http://www.whitehouse.gov/history/presidents

PICTURE CREDITS

INDEX

1850 Compromise, 53–57

A

Adams, John, 33
  administration, 11, 16–17, 22
  campaign, 12, 14
  vice presidency, 10
Adams, John Quincy
  administration, 36, 38
  campaign, 33–34, 36, 40
  as secretary of state, 29, 34
African-Americans, 80
  candidates, 90
  voters, 75, 105
Agnew, Spiro 91
Alien Act, 11
American Civil War, 105
  aftermath, 61
  events leading to, 55, 59–60
American expansion
  as platforms, 25, 29, 50
American Revolution, 25
  aftermath, 9, 22
  debts from, 9–10
  heroes of, 7
Anderson, John, 94

B

Battle of New Orleans, 26–28
Battle of the Thames, 45
Bill of Rights, 9
Blaine, James, 62
Breckinridge, John, 58
Bryan, William Jennings,
  64–65
Buchanan, James, 57
Burr, Aaron
  campaign, 12, 14
  duel with Hamilton, 20
  vice presidency, 14, 19–20

Bush, George H.W.
  administration, 96, 98
  campaign, 96–97, 99
  vice presidency, 96
Bush, George W.
  administration, 103, 105
  campaign, 102–105

C

Calhoun, John C., 51
California, 50, 53, 55, 87
Campaigns, 29
  behind the scenes, 36, 39
  dirty, 14
  influences on, 15
  letter-writing, 12–14
  polls, 72, 77, 94
  primaries, 78, 87, 90
  slogans, 45–46, 48, 65, 73, 98
  and television, 75, 80, 85
  and voters, 16, 22–23, 35, 38–39,
    43, 61, 66, 72, 78, 105
Candidates, presidential
  early, 12–15
  nominations, 34–35, 38, 41,
    45, 54, 57–58, 62–63, 69, 73,
    85
  platforms, 14, 16, 22, 39, 43, 48,
    57, 58–59, 75, 87, 90, 97–98,
    101, 104
  successful, 46
Carter, Jimmy
  administration, 92, 94, 96
  campaign, 91–92
Cass, Lewis, 51, 53
Civilian Conservation Corps, 71
Civil rights, 74
  legislation, 83, 105
  platforms, 75, 77, 79, 81
  prejudice, 61

Clay, Henry
  campaigns, 25, 35–36, 41
  secretary of state, 36–38
Cleveland, Grover, 95
  administration, 63–64
  campaign, 62–63
Clinton, Bill, 105
  administration, 99, 101–102
  campaign, 98–99
  scandals and criticism, 99,
    101–102
Clinton, DeWitt, 26
Clinton, George, 24
  vice president, 21, 23
Communism
  spread of, 75, 77, 79, 81, 85
Congress
  caucus, 38, 44
  control of, 11, 17, 20, 23–25,
    33–34, 36, 57, 85, 92, 99
  debates in, 31, 50
  House of Representatives, 20,
    34–36, 48, 57, 85, 91, 99, 101
  Senate, 34, 66, 85, 99, 102
  special sessions, 70–71
Connally, John, 81
Constitution
  amendments to, 15, 18, 66
  and the election process, 11, 18,
    35
  interpretation of, 43
  and slavery, 31, 57
  and states' rights, 10
  violations of, 12
Continental Army, 9
Continental Congress, 7
Conventions, Democratic, 45
  debates, 64
  divided, 57–59
  establishment of a formal
    national committee, 51, 90
  first, 41
  nominations, 44, 48, 55, 57,
    62–63, 68–69, 79, 85, 87–91,
    94, 98, 104
  restructure, 62, 68, 74, 98–99,
    105–106
  rules and procedures, 41
  violence, 88
Cox, James, 68
Crawford, William, 28, 35–36
Crisholm, Shirley, 90
Cross of Gold speech, 64–66, 68–69
Cuba, 81

D
Daley, Richard, 87
Declaration of Independence,
  104
Democratic Party
  establishment, 41, 43–44
  leadership, 62, 66, 68–69, 76
  modern, 56, 96–106
  new era, 81–82
Democratic-Republicans
  (Republicans)
  formation, 9, 38, 105
  important issues, 9–12, 15,
    22–23, 43
  leadership, 24, 28
  members, 9–12, 14–31
Dewey, Thomas, 74–75, 77
Dixiecrats, 51, 76–77
Douglas, Stephen, 55, 58
Dukakis, Michael, 97

E
Eagleton, Thomas, 90
Eisenhower, Dwight
  administration, 79, 88
  campaign, 78
  war hero, 75
Electoral College
  early years, 14, 18
  importance of, 34
  and popular votes, 35, 43, 63
  vote tallying, 23, 26, 33–36,
    44

F
Federalist Party
  decline of, 15, 26, 28–29, 33
  formation of, 9
  members of, 9–12, 14, 16–18, 21,
    23, 25, 29, 35–36
Ferraro, Geraldine, 96
Fillmore, Millard
  administration, 53–54
  vice presidency, 73
Ford, Gerald, 91
Foreign and domestic policy, 74–75,
  92
  and Monroe, 33
  after the Revolution, 9–10
France
  debts to, 10
  revolution, 12
Free Soil Party, 53–54
Fugitive Slave Act, 54–55

G

Gingrich, Newt, 101
Goldwater, Barry, 85
Gore, Al
    campaign, 102
    vice presidency, 98, 102
Government
    reform, 62
    shaping of, 7, 9–10, 75, 101
    spending, 71, 97
Grant, Ulysses, 61
Great Britain, 50, 57
    conflicts with, 23, 25
    independence from, 7, 9, 22
    at war, 10, 25–28
Great Depression, 68, 70

H

Hamilton, Alexander
    death, 20
    and the Federalists, 9–10
    secretary of treasury, 9
Harding, Warren G., 68
Harrison, Benjamin, 63
Harrison, William Henry, 45, 48
Head Start, 83
Hitler, Adolph, 72
Hoover, Herbert, 68–69
Housing and Urban Development
    Department, 85
Humphrey, Hubert, 75
    campaign, 87–88, 90
Hussein, Saddam, 98, 103

I

Iran hostage crisis, 94–95
Iraq, 103

J

Jackson, Andrew, 29, 50
    administration, 40–46, 105
    campaign, 35–36, 38–40
    and the Democratic-
        Republicans, 38
    war hero, 27–28, 35, 39–40, 45
Jefferson, Thomas
    administration, 14–22, 91
    appointments, 17
    campaigns, 12–14
    and the Democratic-
        Republicans, 9–15, 16–30, 33,
        35, 38, 40, 43, 56, 105
    first inaugural address, 17–19
    issues, 13–15, 22

secretary of state, 9
successor, 22–23
as vice president, 11
vice president, 17–22
Job Corps, 83
Johnson, Andrew
    administration, 61
    vice presidency, 60
Johnson, Lyndon B., 95, 105
    administration, 82, 83, 85–87
    "Great Society," 82–83, 85
    vice presidency, 79

K

Kansas, 55, 57
Kansas-Nebraska Act, 55, 57
Kennedy, John F.
    administration, 80–81, 83, 85
    assassination, 82
    campaign, 78–80
    "New Frontier," 81
Kennedy, Robert, 86
    assassination, 87
Kerry, John, 103–104
King, Martin Luther Jr., 79–80
    assassination, 86
King, Rufus, 29
Korea, 77–78

L

Lane, Joseph, 58
League of Nations, 66
Liberty Party, 47
Lincoln, Abraham
    assassination, 61
    campaign, 59–60, 72
Louisiana Purchase, 22, 32

M

Madison, James, 38, 43
    administration, 25–28, 35
    campaign, 15, 23–26
Maine, 32
Malcolm X, 85
McCarthy, Eugene, 86–87
McClellan, George, 60
McGovern, George, 89–90
McKinley, William, 65
Mentor, Richard, 43
Mexico, 50, 54–55
Military, 54, 66
    campaigns, 98, 103
    desegregation, 76–77
    and Native Americans, 42

Military (continued)
    spending, 96
    state militias, 13–14
    at war, 25–26, 50, 81, 85–91
Missouri Compromise, 31–33, 55
Mondale, Walter, 96–97
Monroe Doctrine, 33–34
Monroe, James, 38, 43
    administration, 29–30, 33–35
    campaign, 15, 23–24, 28
    "Era of Good Feelings," 29

N
National bank, 10, 42, 44
National Republicans, 38, 58
National Union Party, 60
National Unity Party, 94
Native Americans, 42
New Mexico, 50, 53
Nixon, Richard
    administration, 89–91
    campaigns, 78–80, 88–90
    vice presidency, 78
    and Watergate, 90–91

O
Operation Desert Storm, 98
Oregon, 50

P
Peace Corps, 81
Perot, Ross, 98–99
Pierce, Franklin, 55, 57
Political parties
    conventions, 21
    creation of, 7–15, 17, 21
Polk, James, 48, 50
Presidential election of 1796, 11
Presidential election of 1800
    events of, 12–15, 19
Presidential election of 1804,
    17–22
Presidential election of 1808, 15,
    22–23
Presidential election of 1812, 15,
    28–29
Presidential election of 1816, 15
Presidential election of 1820, 15
Presidential election of 1824,
    35–39
Presidential election of 1828, 38–39
Presidential election of 1840, 45–47
Presidential election of 2000, 102
Progressive "Bull Moose" Party, 65

R
Randolph, John, 36–37
Reagan, Ronald
    administration, 95–97
    campaign, 94
Reform Party, 88, 99
Republican Party
    convention, 59
    division in, 65
    formation, 57, 59
    members, 56–57, 59–63, 66,
        72–75, 78, 88, 94–95, 99, 101
    modern, 56, 60
    policies, 68
Republicans. See Democratic-
    Republicans
Roosevelt, Franklin D., 95, 104–105
    administration, 69–74
    campaigns, 68–69, 72–73
    death, 74
    fireside chats, 70–71
    "New Deal," 72, 77
    inaugural speech, 70
Roosevelt, Theodore, 65

S
Sedition Act, 11
September 11 terrorist attacks,
    103–104
Shriver, Sargent, 90
Slavery
    compromises, 53–57
    debates over, 30–31, 47–48, 51,
        57
    and the Democratic Party,
        47–59, 105
    freedom, 62
    laws banning, 31
    lines of division, 31, 50–51,
        53–54
Southern Rights Movements, 51
Soviet Union
    conflicts with, 75, 77, 81, 85, 92
Stevenson, Adlai, 78
Stock market, 64
Supreme Court, 42, 57
    reorganizing, 72
    rulings, 102

T
Taft, William, 65
Talmadge, James, 31
Taylor, Zachary, 54
Tennessee Valley Authority, 71

Texas, 48, 50, 53
Thurmond, Strom, 76–77
Tompkins, Daniel, 28
Transition and turmoil within the
  Democratic Party, 78–81, 87–88
    over presidential candidates,
      35–36
    over slavery, 30, 33, 47–59, 105
    splits within, 26, 38, 51, 53–54,
      57–59
Transportation Department, 85
Treaty of Versailles, 66
Truman, Harry
    administration, 74–78
    campaigns, 76–77
    "fair deal," 77
    inaugural speech, 77
    vice presidency, 74
Twelfth Amendment, 18
Tyler, John, 45, 48

U
United Nations, 77

V
Van Buren, Martin
    administration, 44–45
    campaign, 41–48, 51, 53
    and the Democratic-
      Republicans, 36, 39, 41, 43–44
    vice presidency, 42
Vice President

early elections of, 10–11
    nominations, 17–22
Vietnam War
    United States role in, 81, 83,
      85–91
Voting Rights Act, 85

W
Wallace, George, 88
War
    civil, 60
    with Mexico, 50, 54–55
    and politics, 60–69
War of 1812, 25–28
Washington, D.C.
    burning off, 26–27
    capital in, 17–18
    slave trade in, 53
Washington, George, 22
    cabinet, 7, 9
    first president, 7, 29
Watergate scandal, 90–91
Whig Party
    members, 42, 45–46, 48, 54
Wilkie, Wendell, 73–74
Wilson, Woodrow, 65–66
World War I, 66, 105
World War II, 73, 75

Y
Yarborough, Ralph, 81

ABOUT THE AUTHOR

HEATHER LEHR WAGNER is a writer and an editor. She is the author of more than 30 books exploring social and political issues and focusing on the lives of prominent men and women. She earned a B.A. in political science from Duke University and an M.A. in government from the College of William and Mary. She lives with her husband and family in Pennsylvania.